IT HAPPENED TO ME

Series Editor: Arlene Hirschfelder

Books in the It Happened to Me series are designed for inquisitive teens digging for answers about certain illnesses, social issues, or lifestyle interests. Whether you are deep into your teen years or just entering them, these books are gold mines of up-to-date information, riveting teen views, and great visuals to help you figure out stuff. Besides special boxes highlighting singular facts, each book is enhanced with the latest reading lists, websites, and an index. Perfect for browsing, there are loads of expert information by acclaimed writers to help parents, guardians, and librarians understand teen illness, tough situations, and lifestyle choices.

BIGOTRY AND INTOLERANCE

THE ULTIMATE TEEN GUIDE

KATHLYN GAY

IT HAPPENED TO ME, NO. 35

THE SCARECROW PRESS, INC.
Lanham • Toronto • Plymouth, UK
2013

Published by Scarecrow Press, Inc.
A wholly owned subsidiary of The Rowman & Littlefield Publishing Group, Inc.
4501 Forbes Boulevard, Suite 200, Lanham, Maryland 20706
www.rowman.com

10 Thornbury Road, Plymouth PL6 7PP, United Kingdom

British Library Cataloguing in Publication Information Available

Library of Congress Cataloging-in-Publication Data

Gay, Kathlyn.
 Bigotry and intolerance : the ultimate teen guide / Kathlyn Gay.
   pages cm. — (It happened to me ; no. 35)
 Includes bibliographical references and index.
 ISBN 978-0-8108-8360-4 (cloth : alk. paper) — ISBN 978-0-8108-8361-1 (ebook)
 1. Toleration—Juvenile literature. 2. Toleration—United States—Juvenile literature.
 3. Discrimination—Juvenile literature. 4. Discrimination—United States—Juvenile literature.
 I. Title.
 HM1271.G387 2013
 305.800973—dc23   2012043200

Contents

WHAT'S A BIGOT?

"Bigotry involves verbal abuse that targets people with disabilities and specific sexual orientations, purposely and sometimes inadvertently."
—*Seventeen-year-old Sabrina writing in* Teen Ink[1]

If you pose that question to a dozen people, you are likely to get a dozen different responses. And over the past decade, *bigot* has become a "hot" word and a label directed at politicians, radio and TV talk show hosts, religious leaders, and many others. During the 2012 presidential election campaigns, for example, candidates frequently were called bigots by their opponents. So what *is* a bigot? Dictionaries say a bigot is a person with fixed ideas, one who is "devoted to his or her own opinions and prejudices" and someone who is "strongly partial to his or her own group, religion, race, or politics and intolerant of those who differ." In the early 1800s, Thomas Jefferson, third president of the United States, wrote, "Bigotry is the disease of ignorance, or morbid minds. . . . Education and free discussion are the antidotes of both."[2] For example a bigot might argue, "The world is flat—my Bible says angels held up four corners of the earth and that's what I believe. Period. Read the Bible." You could pull out maps and globes and call attention to geographic explanations about the shape of the earth. But scientific information would not convince someone attached to a flat-earth theory to change her or his mind.

Seventeen-year-old Sabrina responded to the question What's a bigot? by writing in *Teen Ink*, "Bigotry is a term that most teens cannot define, yet take part in daily." She points out that teenagers often use the phrases "That's gay" and "That's retarded" when things don't go their way. She adds, "Bigotry involves verbal abuse that targets people with disabilities and specific sexual orientations, purposely and sometimes inadvertently. . . . Though teens may not realize what they are saying, its [*sic*] time to stop and analyze the discriminatory things they are saying."[3]

Josh, an eighteen-year-old with Down syndrome, knows about disparaging and bigoted remarks. He was featured in 2012 on a Facebook page created by his older sister. Photographs show Josh with a series of printed signs, one pointing out that "some say I have a disability," which prompts people to "sometimes use really mean words" to talk about him. But he holds another sign that says, "These mean words *hurt* but don't describe me at all." Other single-word signs say he is "funny," "loving," "helpful," "smart" and ends with two final statements: "I have feelings just like you and your friends. I'll give you a chance if you give me one, too."[4]

Bigotry in Many Forms

As Josh's signs indicate, he has been stereotyped and would like a chance to just be himself—not prejudged as someone incapable because he has a disability. Stereotypes, prejudice, and discrimination often are the result of fixed ideas about a group of people. Stereotypes and prejudice frequently lead to bigoted ideas and actions. If, for example, older folks have stereotyped notions of teenagers, they might react with fear and even panic if at night they had to pass a group of teenage boys in leather jackets and hoodies. In such an instance, the older individuals have prejudged the group of teenagers, assuming they have violent characteristics.

It is not unusual for a bigoted person to resort to stereotypes such as Asians are sneaky. Blacks are lazy. Hispanics are hot-tempered. Swedes are country bumpkins. Poles are stupid. Lawyers are greedy. Jews are cheap. Muslims are terrorists. Native Americans are alcoholics. Teenagers are irresponsible. Old people are crotchety. Minorities (people of color) are crooks.

For example, in 2011, a Florida resident reported to the sheriff's office that his bicycle was stolen. The deputy responding said in a cavalier manner that the bike was probably taken by one of the "minorities" working on a neighboring construction project. "They don't make much money, you know, and they can sell the bike for a little cash," the deputy said.[5]

ReligiousTolerance.org notes on its website that

> Bigotry . . . is a form of dualism that divides the entire human race into two groups: "us" and "them."
>
> This often results in the rejection or denigration of every member— sight unseen—of an entire group because of a single factor: their age, body shape or weight, caste, color, gender, nationality, race, religion, gender identity, sexual orientation, etc. It is sometimes expressed as a desire or action to deprive an entire group of individuals of fundamental human rights, like freedom of religious expression, or freedom to marry.[6]

In recent times, anyone thought to be a Muslim is suspect and subject to bigoted attacks. Since September 11, 2001, when al-Qaeda members (militant

Islamists) hijacked airplanes and destroyed buildings in the United States, killing thousands, American Muslims, who follow the faith of Islam and the tenets of the Quran, have been vilified as terrorists. The intolerance toward Muslims as a group has created what has been called Islamaphobia—fear of the religion Islam. That fear has resulted in numerous incidents that have threatened the well-being and lives of Muslim Americans, including attacks on mosques in several states, plans to publicly burn the Quran, and protests over the Islamic Center located near the site of New York City's World Trade Center destroyed by terrorists.

In some cases, nonwhites are mistaken for Muslims and threatened with attacks. As an example, one young man of Indian heritage was running toward the Port Authority Bus Station in New York City when someone shouted for a passersby to stop the terrorist. However, the young man, who was not a terrorist by any means, simply kept running. He was in a hurry to catch a bus, and he arrived safely and on time at the station.

Islamaphobia even prompted some Americans to protest a TV reality show titled *All-American Muslim*, which profiled five Muslim families in Dearborn, Michigan, and depicted their rather mundane daily lives. The Florida Family Association (FFA) headed by David Caton managed to convince the home improvement company Lowe's and other sponsors of the reality show to pull their advertising. Caton believes the show is "an inadequate and incomplete image of the Islamic faith" because it does not depict extremists. He told columnist Sue Carlton that ignoring Muslim terrorists "is like The Learning Channel doing a program on pet snakes and failing to include poisonous [ones] and constrictors." Columnist Carlton found that comparing a major world religion to snakes was nonsensical.[7]

Caton and FFA continued their anti-Muslim protests after a Muslim leader was invited by a high school teacher to speak to her class in Hillsborough County in the Tampa Bay, Florida, area. The speaker, Hassan Shibly, heads the Council on American-Islamic Relations (CAIR), and he gives presentations on Islam that fit "the state curriculum that calls for high school students to learn about the world's major religions," the *Tampa Bay Times* reported. But Caton opposes CAIR, contending that it supports extremists. He and his FFA supporters sent more than 2,700 e-mails to the Hillsborough school board in protest. However, the board for the most part backed the high school teacher in her choice of speakers since she invited a variety of religious leaders to make presentations to her class.[8]

Are Bigots Racists?

All bigots are not necessarily racists, but racists are bigots since they often disparage those whose race is different from their own. For example, white racists believe that their particular race is superior to all others. Indigenous people, African Americans, Asian Americans, and others whose skin color differs from the white majority in the United States probably have the longest history of being victimized by racist bigotry.

Of all the physical characteristics, differences in skin color probably had the most impact on how European explorers and settlers in the Americas viewed other groups. No one is certain why individuals have certain reactions to color, but many people have viewed dark colors in a negative manner. The color black, especially, is associated with such negatives as uncleanliness, evil, and death. In stories and film the "good guys" wear white hats and the "bad guys" wear black. Angels appear in white while Satan appears in black. And how about the use of such terms as *blacklisted*, *blackmail*, *black mark*, *black sheep*, and *black deeds*? All have negative associations.

In themselves, negative color connotations would not be enough to keep racial bigotry alive and flourishing. But scientific racism attempted to give credence to the idea that certain races were inferior. It was a way to justify slavery and segregation in the United States. Scientists based their theories on their own views of white supremacy. For example, some scientists believed that different races came from different origins and that only the light-skinned races made significant advances while others remained at "primitive" stages.

After Charles Darwin's theory of evolution was published in the 1800s, American and European intellectuals accepted the idea that humans originated from one source. But they used Darwin's ideas on natural selection to explain social order. Generally, natural selection is the concept that plants and animals respond to changes in the environment (such as climate) by inheritable adaptations or variations that take place over generations. If living things cannot adapt, they die off.

Differences in skin color, for example, might be one way that groups have adapted to climate changes. Dark skin contains large amounts of the pigment melanin, which helps protect the body from ultraviolet rays of the sun. So, theoretically, dark skin might have helped people survive in areas where sunshine and high temperatures are common. Conversely people who migrated to areas with little sun may have developed lighter skin as an adaptation.

Racists, however, have used natural selection concepts to "prove" that a group's achievements are possible because of heredity. In other words, light-skinned people interpreted Darwin's theory to mean that the white race had inherited traits that helped them accomplish more than darker races. Light-skinned people were thought to be higher on the evolutionary ladder than darker-skinned races—and thus superior. Although this type of racism has been around since colonial times in the United States, it has been waning over the past few decades. Still, the belief in white supremacy and statements reflecting racial bigotry prevail.

To cite examples from just one part of the nation—Minnesota—the state's public radio station MPR asked listeners in July 2010, "Do you witness episodes of racial intolerance in your own life?" Numerous responses were posted on Minnesota Public Radio's website. One woman wrote, "I witness racial intolerance AND racism in my daily life. As a white mother of two Latina children I have heard their intelligence and behavior called into question simply because of their skin color. As a teacher I have heard other teachers make comments about students in their classes and their ability to achieve based on their skin color." Another woman posted, "I have experienced racism as a primarily white person. I have heard white people use the 'n' word about our president, I hear people who talk terribly about Native Americans, Mexicans, Latinos, Somalis, Buddhists, Islamics, and Muslims. I have heard people make jokes about shooting Hmongs." Tai Koma posted this, "I have a black hooded jacket that is very shiny, with small pink flowers on it that I was wearing under another winter coat and had anti-Muslim slurs shouted at my back by people who apparently mistook the hood for a headscarf. We were the only ones out at that moment, so I doubt they were yelling at someone else."[9]

In the political arena, biracial President Barack Obama has been portrayed as alien, un-American, and Hitler-like. He has been depicted as a chimpanzee, a suicide bomber, and a pimp. His image has appeared in many other disrespectful, bigoted representations.

Off the Bookshelf

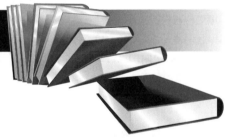

Trouble by Gary D. Schmidt (Boston, New York: Houghton Mifflin Harcourt, 2010) begins with these words: "Henry Smith's father told him that if you build your house far enough away from Trouble, then Trouble will never find you."[10] But, as the description on the paperback edition notes, Trouble finds Henry. "It smashes in the door, taking his brother, destroying his family, and leaving Henry with nothing but a mangy black dog to take care of. So Henry does the only thing he can. He . . . heads for Mt. Katahdin [the highest mountain in Maine], the mountain he wanted to climb with his brother when his brother was still strong and healthy." Henry leaves without telling his parents and takes Black Dog and a friend along for a journey that is not only dangerous but also a time of discovery about his family and heritage.

In April 2011 during a debate on affirmative action in the Oklahoma House of Representatives, Republican Representative Sally Kern of Oklahoma City expressed her opposition. For Kern, affirmative action—taking steps to increase the representation of women and minorities in education, employment, and other areas where they have been excluded—was not necessary. She did not believe it was needed for African Americans because "we have a high percentage of blacks in prison, and that's tragic, but are they in prison just because they are black or because they don't want to study as hard in school? I've taught school, and I saw a lot of people of color who didn't study hard because they said the government would take care of them."[11] She later apologized for her remarks.

In January 2012, Kansas House Speaker Mike O'Neal sent e-mails to some of his colleagues asking them to "Pray for Obama: Psalm 109:8," a slogan that has appeared on bumper stickers and websites. The Psalm says, "May his days be few; may another take his place of leadership." That seems like simply a political point of view. But the next line says, "May his children be fatherless and his wife a widow." It goes on to call for great harm to whomever the psalmist sees as his enemy. This is one of the Psalms in the Bible that expresses deep anger and asks God to invoke a curse on an evil foe. Some argue that the slogan has a bigoted message because it assumes that it is a call for the president's death because of his skin color not his political views.

In addition to O'Neal's Psalm e-mail, he has also sent messages to colleagues that referred to First Lady Michelle Obama as Mrs. YoMama—a term that usually is used to begin an insult: YoMama is a _____ (fill in the slur). He also compared her to Dr. Seuss's Grinch because of a single photo showing Mrs. Obama's hair upswept by the wind in a style similar to Seuss's fictional character. Mrs. Obama's supporters say such comments reflect Speaker O'Neal's bigoted view of black women.

Who Are "America's New Racists"?

According to economics professor Walter E. Williams of George Mason University, blacks as well as whites can be racists. In 2011, he wrote an essay titled "America's New Racists" that was published in numerous conservative magazines and on websites. He described attacks on whites by black youth and mobs of African Americans. Williams recalled that as an African American, he had lived through fearful times when physical assaults on blacks by whites were not only common but often resulted in fatal beatings and lynchings. He argued, "All that has changed. Most racist assaults are committed by blacks." He pointed out that in 2010 "four black Skidmore College students yelled racial slurs while they beat up a white man because he was dining with a black man." That same year, four black girls beat a white girl at a McDonald's, and the victim suffered a seizure. In 2009, "black gangs roamed downtown Denver verbally venting their hatred for white victims before assaulting and robbing them during a two-month crime wave."[12]

Other areas of the country have seen violence perpetrated by blacks against whites. In Wisconsin, for example, the *Milwaukee Journal Sentinel* reported in the summer of 2011 that during the state fair "large groups of African-American youths ran through the midway, knocking over young children and adults, disrupting midway amusement rides and tearing signs up."[13]

On Milwaukee's WTMJ news, witnesses told of white teenagers being beaten by black youth, and an Iraq veteran who was leaving the fair in his car was certain that attacks were racially motivated. He reported, "I had a black couple on my right side, and these black kids were running in between all the cars, and they were pounding on my doors and trying to open up doors on my car, and they didn't do one thing to this black couple that was in this car next to us. They just kept walking right past their car. They were looking in everybody's windshield as they were running by, seeing who was white and who was black."[14]

"Racist black attacks are not only against whites but also against Asians," Professor Williams wrote. He cited these instances:

In San Francisco, five blacks beat an 83-year-old Chinese man to death. They threw a 57-year-old woman off a train platform. Two black Oakland teenagers assaulted a 59-year-old Chinese man; the punching knocked him to the ground, killing him. At Philly's South Philadelphia High School, Asian students report that black students routinely pelt them with food and beat, punch and kick them in school hallways and bathrooms as they hurl racial epithets such as "Hey, Chinese!" and "Yo, Dragon Ball!"

For Williams, "Black silence in the face of black racism has to be one of the biggest betrayals of the civil rights struggle that included black and white Americans."[15]

In spite of news stories describing racial bigotry among African Americans, many pundits would argue that black racism is nothing like white racism. For one thing, racism has been institutionalized in the United States. That is, there are political, economic, and social policies that provide benefits for white Americans at the expense of nonwhite racial and ethnic groups. It occurs when corporations, governments, universities, and other institutions discriminate, either deliberately or indirectly, against certain groups of people to limit their rights. It reflects the cultural assumptions of the dominant group, so that the practices of that group are seen as the norm to which other cultural practices should conform. Institutional racism is more subtle, less visible, and less identifiable than individual acts of racism, but it is no less destructive to human life and human dignity. A group called Solid Ground working to end poverty in King County, Washington, notes,

> In the United States, institutional racism has been responsible for slavery, settlement, Indian reservations, segregation, residential schools (for American Indians), and internment camps. While most of these institutions no longer exist, they have had long-term impacts on our society. As a result . . . racial stratification and disparities have occurred in employment, housing, education, healthcare, government and other sectors. While many laws were passed in the mid-20th century to make discrimination illegal, major inequalities still exist. Institutional racism is distinguished from the bigotry or racial bias of individuals by the existence of systematic policies and practices within institutions that effectually disadvantage certain racial or ethnic groups. Institutional racism can only exist in institutions where the power to enforce and perpetuate policies and practices is invested in white people.[16]

One powerful example of the impact of institutional racism is the fact that for much of U.S. history, the white majority for the most part deemed it acceptable to have unfavorable stereotypes of people of color, which resulted in widespread discrimination and racist hate groups like the Ku Klux Klan that spread terror and lynched black people.

Federal Bureau of Investigation (FBI) hate crime statistics released in November 2011 show that in 2010, U.S. law enforcement agencies reported 6,628 hate incidents. The FBI states, "A hate crime is a traditional offense like murder, arson, or vandalism with an added element of bias. For the purposes of collecting statistics, Congress has defined a hate crime as a 'criminal offense against a person or property motivated in whole or in part by an offender's bias against a race, religion, disability, ethnic origin or sexual orientation.'"[17] The FBI identified the races of the 6,008 known hate crime offenders. Of those, 58.6 percent were white and 18.4 percent were black. Almost 9 percent were groups made up of individuals of various races, 1.1 percent were Asian/Pacific Islander, 1.0 percent were American Indian/Alaskan Native, and the race of 12 percent was unknown.[18]

Weight Prejudice

When Christianne was a young teenager, she weighed 180 pounds and faced daily taunts and jeers from classmates. "Kids at school called me stupid things like 'tub of lard' or 'fatty.' Some kids would yell 'Moo,'" she told a *Choices* reporter, adding, "It really hurt."[19]

"I was a fat kid and I am a fat adult," wrote Lee, a young woman in her twenties. "For a brief but oh-so-amazing period in junior high, after I went to camp and played tennis and walked everywhere and rode horses and swam twelve hours a day, I was what everyone seemed to consider slender." But when she was in high school things changed. As Lee reported,

> I took up more space than the Levi's girls, the ones with the sleek size 2's that would fit only one of my legs and the Izod shirts that hung straight and clean over bellies that didn't pooch, not even a little bit. I didn't play sports because fat girls didn't play sports. I was in band because there were fat kids coming out of the woodwork in band. The true love of my life . . . was/is books. The only gripe I have with books: Where are the fat spies? Where are the fat sexy princesses? The fat cops, portrayed in a good light? The fat righters of wrongs, exposers of evil, vindicators? The fat *anyone* not drawn as a lazy, corrupted, sneering s.o.b. with only one thing on his/her mind—cheeseburgers?"[20]

These complaints reflect the prejudice against a fat person that is all too common for children and adults who happen to weigh more than what is considered "normal" for their peers. As Sondra Solovay, an expert on weight-based legal issues, wrote, "Fat children and teens suffer serious discrimination. . . . Abuse of fat kids both during and outside of school hours is an everyday occurrence. It is generally neither seen nor treated as a problem by the courts, nor taken seriously by the school's staff. But it is a serious problem."[21]

Solovay and many other writers have described the kind of humiliation fat students face in sports and gym classes. They frequently are ridiculed, boycotted from team sports, told publicly that they need to diet, harassed physically, and intimidated or attacked by bullies. In locker rooms and showers, fat students are especially vulnerable to derision since they do not have the protection of clothing or of adult authority figures such as teachers and coaches.

Issues of weight have become highly publicized in recent years as medical experts warn the public about the health dangers of obesity. Dr. Reginald Washington of the U.S. Centers for Disease Control and Prevention (CDC) notes that "although the effects of obesity on the physical health of children are well documented, the emotional and social consequences of obesity are less detailed and not as well understood, and therefore are often ignored. The emotional consequences of obesity include low self-esteem, negative body image, and clinical depression."[22]

Overweight people frequently are subjected to bigoted comments and behavior.

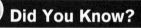

> **Did You Know?**
>
> "*Weight bias* can be defined as the inclination to form unreasonable judgments based on a person's weight. *Stigma* is the social sign that is carried by a person who is a victim of prejudice and weight bias," according to the CDC.[23]

When Bigots Target Short People

While weight bias appears to be more prevalent than height bias (called height-ism), many people of short stature can describe incidents they have experienced as targets of bigotry, particularly in their teenage years. They are taunted with names such as "small fry," "shrimp," "pea brain," "elf," "runt," "munchkin," "shorty," "pip-squeak," "peanut," or "spear-chucker." The latter is a "derogatory term for African pygmies that hunted with spears," according to author and

It Happened to Nineteen-Year-Old Darren Millan

"Some people think I'm only good for the circus," Darren, a Glasgow University student in England told a British reporter. But Darren, who has achondroplasia, or dwarfism, is an exceptional student, next to the top of his class. At four feet, two inches, he is subjected to stares, name-calling, and other abuse on a daily basis. "It's a five-minute laugh" to his bigoted taunters, and that "used to upset me for the whole day," he reported. But his parents, who also have achondroplasia, taught him "how to handle situations." Darren attended meetings of the Restricted Growth Association (similar to the Little People of America organization). There he "was in a place with people who were all the same height as me. I could look everyone in the eye. Now I've got dwarf mates and tall mates and I'm comfortable and confident with all of them. I know I'm able to pretty much do whatever I like."[24] Darren also expressed appreciation for popular comedian Verne Troyer, an American who is less than three feet tall and has shown that little people can succeed in films and television. Verne, who is in his forties, has appeared in more than a dozen movies and is a role model for young adults like Darren.

sociologist Deborah J. Burris-Kitchen, who wrote *Short Rage: An Autobiographical Look at Heightism in America*.[25] In her book, Burris-Kitchen describes what it has been like to be four feet, nine inches tall and to be patronized, overlooked, and underestimated because she is short.

Short-statured youths have been plagued with insulting jokes or demeaning stunts like being stuffed into a locker, or they have suffered condescending remarks from people who view them as less than intelligent because of their size. Heightism can have a direct effect on a short person's income, social life, and relationships, according to award-winning journalist Stephen Hall, who as a teenager was shorter than 99 percent of his classmates. Hall points out in his book *Size Matters: How Height Affects the Health, Happiness, and Success of Boys—and the Men They Become* that there is a "cultural obsession with height."[26] He writes, "Countless social science surveys have shown that the public uncritically ascribes positive traits to tall people—more intelligent, more likable, more dependable, and better leaders" than short people.[27]

Except for a brief historical reference, Hall does not discuss the type of bigotry that people with achondroplasia (dwarfism) experience. Achondroplasia is the most common of the two hundred types of dwarfism, and usually a person with achondroplasia grows no taller than four feet, ten inches. Dwarfed teens and adults, who often refer to themselves as little people, have been stereotyped throughout history as curiosities, comic figures, trolls, fairy-tale creatures capable of evil, or in the worst cases as "freaks." Today, dwarfism is commonly equated with mental retardation and the inability to perform well in the "real" world. But the fact is that dwarfism has nothing to do with intelligence and that people with achondroplasia have done well in school and as adults in numerous jobs and professions.

Consider Caleb Tourres of Jefferson Parish, Louisiana, who was born with achondroplasia. He was a high school junior in 2007, standing four feet, two inches. He graduated from Archbishop Rummel High School with honors in 2008. While still in school, some of his accomplishments included acting roles in school plays, membership in Big Brothers, manager of the high school basketball team, and winner of one of the top slots as a power lifter in the school's weight lifting team. No stranger to derogatory remarks about his size, Tourres explains, "When I go to meets, you hear some mumblings like 'What is he doing there?' or kids will say, 'Look, it's a midget.'" The term *midget* is highly offensive to people with achondroplasia because it is associated with freak shows when little people were displayed for public amusement. Still, Tourres brushes off the insults "because [he] understand[s] where people are coming from when they see somebody that's not like them."[28]

Most if not all dwarfed individuals have experienced comments such as Tourres describes. But unlike Tourres, many little people find it difficult to ignore insults, teasing, and harassment. One woman recalling her teen years notes, "I thought I was prepared when I went to high school. I knew that other people thought I was strange with my short arms and legs, but one boy really shocked me. He came up to me in the hall and asked, 'When are you going to join the circus?' I was upset all day. Just because I'm different doesn't mean I'm a freak!"[29]

Actor Peter Dinklage, who was born with achondroplasia, explains, "When I was younger, definitely, I let it [being dwarfed] get to me." Dinklage attended school in Morristown, New Jersey, and notes, "As an adolescent, I was bitter and angry and I definitely put up these walls. But the older you get, you realize you just have to have a sense of humor. You just know that it's not your problem. It's theirs."[30] Dinklage began his acting career in New York City but he refused to play roles that stereotyped and made fun of dwarfed people. His first major role was in the 2003 film *The Station Agent*. He won an Emmy award and Golden Globe in 2011 for best supporting actor in the HBO series *Game of Thrones*.

Dwarf Tossing—What Do You Think?

In October 2011, Representative Ritch Workman, a Florida state legislator, introduced a bill to repeal a law that bans dwarf tossing, which was outlawed in 1989. Dwarf tossing is a competition that usually takes place in a bar. A dwarf wears protective gear and a harness and patrons take turns throwing a dwarf against a padded wall or onto a mattress. The activity is considered a "sport" by some bar owners and customers in the United States and Canada and also in Great Britain and New Zealand where it is legal. It has been popular entertainment in some U.S. college hangouts as well. But to many people this type of entertainment represents a form of bigotry because it dehumanizes the dwarfed person.

Yet, a small number of little people who earn income by being tossed consider it their right to participate. In the view of the Florida legislator, "If this is a job they want and people would pay to see it or participate in it, then the law banning it should be repealed."[31] A Florida radio personality called Dave the Dwarf, who is a little more than three feet tall, argues that he, not the government, should decide what he can do with his body.

Little People of America (LPA), a national organization that advocates for people of short stature, strongly argues that the ban on dwarf tossing should remain because the competition contributes to stereotypes of dwarfs—that is, dwarfs are seen as objects like footballs or throwaways. In addition, tossing a dwarf is dangerous. As a LPA spokesperson told the *Huffington Post*, "There are orthopedic and neurological complications associated with many forms of dwarfism, [and] the person being tossed is at high risk of back and neck injury."[32]

So what do you think? Is dwarf tossing a form of bigotry? Should laws forbid dwarf tossing or should such laws be repealed?

Notes

1. Sabrina, "Think before You Speak," *Teen Ink*, n.d. www.teenink.com/opinion/discrimination/article/157772/Bigotry-Think-Before-You-Speak/ (accessed January 18, 2012).

2. Thomas Jefferson, "Quotation by Thomas Jefferson," Dictionary.com Quotes, n.d. quotes. dictionary.com/bigotry_is_the_disease_of_ignorance_of_morbid (accessed December 6, 2012).

3. Sabrina, "Think before You Speak."

4. Grace Estelle Curley, "Messsage to Alll My FB Friends! Look at Pictures in Order," Facebook, January 2012, www.facebook.com/media/set/?set=a.10150341805178388.343953.5114 03387&type=3 (accessed January 21, 2012).

5. Officer's unsolicited comment directed to the author, September 2011.

6. Ontario Consultants on Religious Tolerance, "A New English Word: 'Religism,' Which Means Bigotry Based on Religious Belief," ReligiousTolerance.org, last updated November 29, 2011, www.religioustolerance.org/religism.htm (accessed January 21, 2012).

7. Sue Carlton, "Outrage at Muslim Show Is Contrived," *St. Petersburg Times*, December 21, 2011, 1B.

8. Marlene Sokol, "Critic's Followers Take Up Causes," *Tampa Bay Times*, January 11, 2012, 10B.

9. Eric Ringham, "Do You Witness Episodes of Racial Intolerance in Your Own Life?" *MPRNews*, July 12, 2010, minnesota.publicradio.org/collections/special/columns/todays -question/archive/2010/07/do-you-witness-episodes-of-racial-intolerance-in-your-own-life .shtml (accessed January 31, 2012).

10. Gary D. Schmidt, *Trouble* (Boston: Houghton Mifflin Harcourt, 2010), 1.

11. LaFeminista, "Deep-Rooted Racial Bigotry in Oklahoma," *Daily Kos* (blog), April 28, 2011, www.dailykos.com/story/2011/04/28/971125/-Deep-Rooted-Racial-Bigotry-in-Oklahoma (accessed January 25, 2012).

12. Walter E. Williams, "America's New Racists," *Townhall.com*, June 22, 2011, townhall.com/ columnists/walterewilliams/2011/06/22/americas_new_racists/page/full/ (accessed January 25, 2012).

13. Don Walker, Mike Johnson, and Breann Schossow, "State Fair Melees Produce 11 Injuries, 31 Arrests," *Milwaukee Journal Sentinel*, August 5, 2011, www.jsonline.com/news/milwaukee/ 126828998.html (accessed January 25, 2011).

14. WTMJ News Team, "Witnesses Describe Mobs, Some People Claim Racially-Charged Attacks," *TodaysTMJ4.com*, August 5, 2011, www.todaystmj4.com/news/local/126825018.html (accessed January 26, 2012).

15. Williams, "America's New Racists."

16. Solid Ground, "Definition & Analysis of Institutional Racism," n.d., www.solid-ground .org/Programs/Legal/AntiRacism/Documents/ARI_Definitions-Accountability_Standards_ ONLINE_7-09.pdf (accessed October 5, 2012).

17. Federal Bureau of Investigation, "Hate Crime Overview," Civil Rights section, n.d., www .fbi.gov/about-us/investigate/civilrights/hate_crimes/overview (accessed January 27, 2012).

18. Federal Bureau of Investigation, "Offenders," *Hate Crime Statistics, 2010*, released November 14, 2011, www.fbi.gov/about-us/cjis/ucr/hate-crime/2010/narratives/hate-crime -2010-offenders.pdf (accessed January 27, 2012).

19. Denise Rinaldo, "Weight War," *Choices*, April–May 2004, 8.

20. Lee, quoted in "School," I Was a Fat Kid . . . This Is My Story, n.d., www.catay.com/fatkid/ school.asp (accessed January 29, 2012).

21. Sondra Solovay, *Tipping the Scales of Justice: Fighting Weight-Based Discrimination* (Amherst, NY: Prometheus Books, 2000), 33.

22. Reginald L. Washington, "Childhood Obesity: Issues of Weight Bias," *Preventing Chronic Disease* 8, no.5 (September 2011), www.cdc.gov/pcd/issues/2011/sep/10_0281.htm (accessed January 29, 2012).

23. Washington, "Childhood Obesity."

24. Lesley Roberts, "Some People Think I'm Only Good for the Circus. We Need Role Models Like Verne," *DailyRecord.co.uk*, January 11, 2009, www.dailyrecord.co.uk/archive/2009/01/11/some-people-think-i-m-only-good-for-the-circus-we-need-role-models-like-verne-78057-21031864/ (accessed February 5, 2012).

25. Deborah J. Burris-Kitchen, *Short Rage: An Autobiographical Look at Heightism in America* (Santa Barbara, CA: Fithian Press, 2002), 20.

26. Stephen S. Hall, *Size Matters: How Height Affects the Health, Happiness, and Success of Boys—and the Men They Become* (Boston and New York: Houghton Mifflin, 2006), 12.

27. Hall, *Size Matters*, 15.

28. Kathlyn Gay, *Body Image and Appearance: The Ultimate Teen Guide* (Lanham, MD: Scarecrow Press, 2009), 81.

29. Anonymous, interview with the author, 1999.

30. IMDb staff, "Biography for Peter Dinklage," Internet Movie Database, n.d., www.imdb.com/name/nm0227759/bio (accessed February 5, 2012).

31. Bloomberg News, "Dwarfs Better Off Tossed Than Jobless, Florida Lawmaker Says," *St. Petersburg Times*, October 8, 2011, B2.

32. David Moye, "Dwarf Tossing Legalization: Some Little People Support Repealing Florida Law," *Huffington Post*, updated December 6, 2011, www.huffingtonpost.com/2011/10/06/possible-dwarf-tossing-repeal-big-news-to-little-people_n_998878.html (accessed February 4, 2012).

WIDESPREAD BIGOTRY AND INTOLERANCE

....

*"Since I was younger I . . . considered being lighter as a form of beauty or
you know, more beautiful than being dark-skinned, so I used to think of myself as
being ugly because I was dark-skinned."*—*Eighteen-year-old Jennifer
in the documentary* A Girl Like Me[1]

Teen filmmaker Kiri Davis created the documentary *A Girl Like Me*, inter-
viewing her African American peers to determine how racism, the color of
their skin, and the texture of their hair have affected them. One teenager said,
"I remember when I first started wearing my hair natural, at first my mom was
ok with it and she thought it looked nice. And then after like the second day, she
was like, 'oh stop that.' She was like, 'you're starting to look African.' I was like,
'well, I am African.' And that really pissed me off."

Eighteen-year-old Glenda noted, "There are standards that are imposed upon
us, like, you know, you're pretty, you're prettier if you're light-skinned."

Jennifer, age eighteen, said, "My siblings are all lighter than me and my mom,
she [is] dark-skinned, but she's lighter than me. So like I noticed and I was like,
'hey, how come I'm the darkest and you know everybody else is so light?'"[2]

Skin color long has been a point of contention in discussions and arguments
over racism and discriminatory actions against dark-skinned nonwhite people in
the United States. As an old saying put it, "If you're white, you're all right; if
you're yellow, you're mellow; if you're brown, stick around; if you're black, step
back." In other words, people have been divided by skin color, which has determined their race and status.

Racial categories can create heated debate because there is no universal agreement on how or if humans should be classified. In the first place, every classification system has been devised by a person with a particular point of view based
on a specific discipline such as anthropology or biology. Although racial classification systems have varied considerably over the years, there is agreement that all

people belong to one species—*Homo sapiens*. Gordon Allport pointed out years ago in his classic work *The Nature of Prejudice* that "(1) Except in remote parts of the earth very few human beings belong to a pure stock; most [humans] are mongrels (racially speaking). . . . (2) Most human characteristics ascribed to race are undoubtedly due to cultural diversity and should, therefore, be regarded as ethnic, not racial."[3]

In 1998, the American Anthropological Association issued a statement on "race," declaring that the term did not refer to a biological construct—that is, skin color, hair texture, facial features, and so forth—but instead "race" is a social concept. The association refers to "race" in quotation marks because

> today scholars in many fields argue that "race" as it is understood in the United States of America was a social mechanism invented during the 18th century to refer to those populations brought together in colonial America: the English and other European settlers, the conquered Indian peoples, and those peoples of Africa brought in to provide slave labor. . . . As they were constructing US society, leaders among European-Americans fabricated the cultural/behavioral characteristics associated with each "race," linking superior traits with Europeans and negative and inferior ones to blacks and Indians. Numerous arbitrary and fictitious beliefs about the different peoples were institutionalized and deeply embedded in American thought.

The association statement concludes,

> How people have been accepted and treated within the context of a given society or culture has a direct impact on how they perform in that society. The "racial" worldview was invented to assign some groups to perpetual low status, while others were permitted access to privilege, power, and wealth. The tragedy in the United States has been that the policies and practices stemming from this worldview succeeded all too well in constructing unequal populations among Europeans, Native Americans, and peoples of African descent. Given what we know about the capacity of normal humans to achieve and function within any culture, we conclude that present-day inequalities between so-called "racial" groups are not consequences of their biological inheritance but products of historical and contemporary social, economic, educational, and political circumstances.[4]

Prominent biologist E. O. Wilson posits that humans are divided because of tribal loyalty: "Everyone, no exception, must have a tribe, an alliance with which to jockey for power and territory, to demonize the enemy, to organize rallies and raise flags," he writes in the *Daily Beast*, adding,

And so it has ever been. In ancient history and prehistory, tribes gave visceral comfort and pride from familiar fellowship, and a way to defend the group enthusiastically against rival groups. It gave people a name in addition to their own and social meaning in a chaotic world. It made the environment less disorienting and dangerous. Human nature has not changed. Modern groups are psychologically equivalent to the tribes of ancient history. As such, these groups are directly descended from the bands of primitive humans and prehumans.[5]

Wilson points out in his article how experiments over the years have shown that even when random groups are formed, prejudice quickly becomes apparent. People "discriminate in favor of the one to which they belong . . . participants always ranked the out-group below the in-group. They judged their 'opponents' to be less likable, less fair, less trustworthy, less competent. The prejudices asserted themselves even when the subjects were told the in-groups and out-groups had been chosen arbitrarily."[6]

Classifying Humans

In the 1700s, a Swedish biologist, Carl Linnaeus, published his *Systema Naturae*, which categorized animals by Latin names and included *Homo sapiens*, or humans, in the animal kingdom. Linnaeus divided humans into four subcategories called *Homo sapiens americanus*, *Homo sapiens europaeus*, *Homo sapiens asiaticus*, and *Homo sapiens afer*. Under each group he listed characteristics that he declared distinguished one race from another—skin color, hair, and facial features among them. Others included judgmental statements about each color group. Linnaeus claimed the red group was resolute, cheerful, free; the whites were nimble, of the keenest mind; the pale yellow group was grave, proud, greedy; and the black group was cunning, lazy, careless.

Another classifying method used in the eighteenth and nineteenth centuries was based on craniology, a pseudoscience also called phrenology that studied people's skulls. Head shape and size, bulges, and depressions were measured carefully to determine individuals' mental abilities, personality characteristics, and intelligence. The findings were used to differentiate between groups of people and to support the superiority of whites.

People of "Mixed" Heritage

Racial/color categories were also used to rank and classify offspring of interracial unions. For example, *half-breed* was the common term for someone of Caucasian and Native American heritage. But the categories were particularly insulting for progeny of black-white unions. During the 1800s, anyone of half Caucasian (white) and half African American heritage was commonly labeled *mulatto* (from the Spanish *mulato* from *mula* meaning "mule"—one-half horse and one-half donkey, or a hybrid). Other terms followed: *quadroon* for one-fourth black; *octoroon* for one-eighth black; *griffe* for one-sixteenth black; and other terms to identify someone with even one-sixty-fourth black heritage. The use of such terms continued well into the twentieth century, particularly mulatto, which is still applied on occasion today.

The absurdity of the classification system is apparent when you consider that it is impossible to measure any precise fraction of a person's heritage. Consider just one example: Someone is said to be one-sixteenth black and ten-sixteenths white. Logically that person would be labeled white. But the classification system was not designed to be logical. It was the basis for what is commonly known as the one-drop-of-black-blood rule. In white supremacist jargon that meant that a person with any portion of black heritage no matter how small the fraction was "inferior." Through the years African Americans also have applied the one-drop rule, arguing that anyone with black blood should call himself or herself black. Yet, genes, not blood, are the biological units that transmit hereditary traits.

When Audra Johnson was a teenager in Indiana, she talked about her blended traits—her father is of German heritage and her mother is of Cherokee and black ancestry. "When people ask about my background I always tell them I'm mixed, even though they usually want to label me 'black.' I am part black, and I am also part white. I refuse to pick sides for anyone. I am who I am, and until people decide to change their narrow-minded view of the world, I am just going to have to continue to remind them."[7]

Dividing by Caste and Ethnicity

Mention the terms *bigotry* and *intolerance* and many in Western culture today think of whites enslaving African Americans and indigenous people. But in ancient Greece and Rome, race was not a factor—"both blacks and whites were slaves," writes Harvard professor Frank Snowden Jr., "but blacks and slaves were never synonymous." Blacks who emigrated to Mediterranean lands "were not excluded from opportunities available to others of alien extraction, nor were they handicapped in fundamental social relations—they were physically and culturally assimilated."[8] However, ancient Greeks and Romans were divided by class or caste with roles determined by their places in society. In the caste system, there were groups considered "civilized" and others called "barbarians," who were subject to enslavement.

No one knows how many slaves were held in all of ancient Greece, but an estimated one hundred thousand slaves "labored in Athens during the fourth and fifth centuries B.C., or at least three or four slaves for each free household. This is a proportion of the population much larger than that of the slave states in America on the eve of the Civil War," according to historian David E. Stannard.[9]

Throughout history, many groups of people have claimed superiority over other cultures and have labeled strangers barbarians, which often simply meant not being part of the in-group. Some civilizations, such as ancient Egyptians, considered themselves more human than any foreigners they encountered. Romans who conquered Greece believed they were far superior to those they ruled. Most conquerors, in fact, have believed that their ways were best.

Later, in feudal societies, people were divided into distinct classes. Merchants, commoners, and slaves were on the lowest rungs of the social ladder. They were expected to provide food, shelter, clothing, weapons, and other needed items for the knights, lords, and the king.

Whatever the division within a society, people were nevertheless bonded by common customs and language. It was not unusual to have an *ethnocentric* belief—that is, believing one's own ethnic, or cultural, group is better than others. Ethnocentric belief prompted the ancient Chinese, for example, to claim they were unique among early civilizations. Anyone who did not speak their language was considered a barbarian. Outsiders, even conquerors, were expected to adopt Chinese customs.

The Japanese also thought they were unique and that their nation should be kept ethnically "pure." In their view, ethnic bonds such as language, traditions, and religious practices should be maintained. In Japan, conformity and being loyal to one's group have been prized (and expected) characteristics. And most people have conformed. If not, as the saying goes, "The protruding nail gets hammered down." Students who show streaks of individualism have been taunted, bullied, and even brutally attacked for being "different." Even in the late twentieth century, being a nonconformist student in Japan could be "dangerous," as the *Boston Globe* put it. The newspaper reported 4,854 physical attacks and thirteen deaths of Japanese students, nearly all related to bullying. For example, a teenage girl was systematically taunted and finally attacked and killed because she "dressed poorly" in school uniforms that had been handed down from her older sister. One of the girl's assailants said that wearing a used uniform was an "irritation" to "all other students [who] have new uniforms each year."[10]

Students in Japan are expected to conform and wear school uniforms.

Early American Ethnocentrism

From the 1400s through the 1600s, European explorers and conquerors had little regard for the peoples they encountered in Asia, Africa, and the Americas. Europeans returned home with stories that clearly showed their bias against or even hatred of people who differed from themselves. Frequently they referred to Africans and indigenous Americans as "savages" or as "subhumans."

By accepting an ethnocentric view, light-skinned people could rationalize and justify subordinating darker-skinned peoples. In fact, European conquerors and colonists did just that. They claimed land and grabbed mineral wealth while forcing original populations in South America into slave labor and killing off thousands of indigenous people in both North and South America. In the process of establishing colonies, Europeans also exploited countless people in Asia and Africa, and they captured millions of Africans to be sold into slavery.

At the same time, Christianity played a role in reinforcing ethnocentric ideas. Many, but by no means all, Christian leaders in Europe and in the American colonies believed that Africans and Native Americans were pagans and not fit for anything except serving so-called superior whites. That view became strongly entrenched as colonists needed labor to develop the land and build towns and cities. By justifying slavery on the basis of the victims' subhuman status, many early settlers adamantly defended slave trade. Some were even convinced that slavery would help bring salvation to the "heathens" and that slaves were happy because they had been rescued from barbarism and were provided with food and shelter. The fact that Africans lived in well-developed agricultural societies meant little or nothing to slave captors.

Ethnocentrism remained strong among the early American colonists, the vast majority of whom were light-skinned Protestants (Anglos) from Britain and northern European countries. They wanted to maintain the way of life in their original homelands, even though many eventually rebelled and fought for independence during the American Revolution. As John Jay noted in *The Federalist Papers* (written to explain the new Constitution of the United States), the people of the proposed new nation were a "united people—a people descended from the same ancestors, speaking the same language, professing the same religion, attached to the same principles of government, very similar in their manners and customs."[11]

Although "professing the same religion," Protestant groups in the colonies were diverse in their beliefs and often in conflict. However, they were united in their prejudice against the Roman Catholic minority. In Maryland, for example, Catholics were denied political rights and were forbidden to hold religious services in public. Colonists also discriminated against Jews, barring them from voting in most colonies.

With the development of the new nation and the industrial revolution that followed, more and more people were needed to populate the land and work in the factories and fields. By the mid-1800s there was a great influx of newcomers. Many were Catholic immigrants from Germany and Ireland who were not warmly greeted. Citizens born in the United States resented the new immigrants. They believed the Germans and Irish were aliens who would pollute their so-called pure and native stock. Nativists, as they became known, also resented the Germans and

Irish for their clannishness and for preserving their customs, such as boisterous drinking habits. Irish workers were especially scorned because of fear that they would take nativists' jobs. Many factory and shop owners hung out signs saying, "No Irish Need Apply."

Acting on their ethnocentric views, nativists called for restrictions on immigration, wrote books and pamphlets urging Protestants to fight the "Catholic menace," and incited anti-Catholic riots. Secret nativist societies sprang up, and eventually a national organization called the Supreme Order of the Star-Spangled Banner was formed. Members swore to secrecy and when asked about their activities would say, "I know nothing," earning them the moniker Know-Nothings.

Eventually, the Know-Nothings formed a political party, but they gained little political strength and the party split over slavery. However, their antiforeignism flourished as immigrants continued to come from Europe, Asia, Mexico, and other parts of the world. Laws were passed by the U.S. Congress to limit the number of some immigrant groups, such as the Chinese and Japanese.

Many Americans were especially prejudiced against Chinese immigrants who arrived in the 1800s to work in the gold mines, on the railroads, and in agriculture, settling by the thousands in California. In *The Annals of San Francisco*, the authors wrote in 1854, "The manners and habits of the Chinese are very repugnant to Americans in California." The discussion continued to note that

the Chinaman is looked upon by some as only a little superior to the negro, and by others as somewhat inferior. It is needless to reason upon such a matter. Those who have mingled familiarly with "celestials" [natives of China] have commonly felt before long an uncontrollable sort of loathing

? Did You Know?

Economic and political considerations are major factors in the perpetuation of ethnocentrism, bigotry, and prejudice. Ethnocentrism persists in order to maintain the status quo, or the social structure that exists. In the United States, the white male majority holds most of the political power and also controls most of the large corporations and businesses. It is not likely that people within that power structure will voluntarily give up their advantages and privileged positions. As a result, when anyone not part of the power structure tries to gain economic or political influence, he or she may be seen as a threat, so an "outsider" may be denied opportunities for advancement.

against them. [A Chinaman] does not smell very sweetly; his color and the features of his face are unusual; his penuriousness is extreme; his lying, knavery and natural cowardice are proverbial; he dwells apart from white persons, herding only with countrymen, unable to communicate his ideas to such as are not of his nation, or to show the better part of his nature. He is poor and mean, somewhat slavish and crouching, and is despised by the whites, who would only laugh in derision if even a divine were to pretend to place the two races on an equality. In short, there is a strong feeling—prejudice it may be—existing in California against all Chinamen, and they are nicknamed, cuffed about and treated very unceremoniously by every other class.[12]

The type of prejudice against the Chinese in the United States is not only a form of ethnocentrism but also a type of institutionalized racism—the majority of white Americans felt it was acceptable to have unfavorable opinions of a group different from themselves. When such opinions become part of the social and economic fabric of a nation, widespread discrimination results. Certainly that was the case with the kind of racism that kept African Americans enslaved until the Civil War period and that for generations afterward provoked widespread discrimination against blacks.

When the United States entered World War II after the Japanese attack on the American military base at Pearl Harbor in 1941, a form of institutionalized racism took hold. Lieutenant General John L. DeWitt, who was in charge of the U.S. Western Defense Command, sent a memo to Secretary of War Henry L. Stimson recommending the evacuation of all Japanese Americans from the coastal areas of California, Oregon, and the state of Washington. DeWitt wrote,

The Japanese race is an enemy race and while many second and third generation Japanese, born on United States soil, possessed of United States citizenship have become Americanized, the racial strains are undiluted. . . . It therefore follows that along the Pacific Coast over 112,000 potential enemies of Japanese extraction are at large today. To conclude otherwise is to expect that children born of white parents on Japanese soil sever all racial affinity and become loyal Japanese subjects, ready to fight and, if necessary, to die for Japan in a war against the nation of their parents. That Japan is allied with Germany and Italy in this struggle is no ground for assuming that any Japanese, barred from assimilation by convention as he is, though born and raised in the United States, will not turn against this nation when the final test of loyalty comes. It, therefore, follows that along the vital Pacific Coast over 112,000 potential enemies, of Japanese extraction, are at large today.[13]

It Happened to Yuri Kochiyama

On the day Pearl Harbor was bombed, twenty-one-year-old Yuri Kochiyama, daughter of Japanese immigrants who settled in San Pedro, California, was in church where she taught Sunday school. Yuri's father owned and operated a market that sold fish, meat, and other supplies to the U.S. Navy and Japanese passenger ships that sailed between Japan and the West Coast of the United States. "Our home life was traditional in that we spoke Japanese and ate Japanese food and were expected to behave as proper Japanese children. Outside our home though I was very much an 'all-American' girl,'" Yuri wrote.[14]

A few hours after she returned home from church on December 7, 1941, Federal Bureau of Investigation (FBI) agents arrived. The agents quickly took away Yuri's father, who had just returned from the hospital after having surgery. Although he had committed no crime, he was a Japanese immigrant and a man in contact with Japanese fishermen who knew the waters of the Pacific Ocean, so without any evidence, he, like other Issei (first-generation Japanese), was accused of spying for Japan. He was imprisoned on Terminal Island, where he was denied the medication he needed for diabetes. He was not allowed to have visitors except for his son Peter (Yuri's twin brother), who had been drafted into the U.S. Army. The elder Kochiyama became so ill that he had to be hospitalized and then was sent home in such poor condition that he died on January 21, 1942. Yuri learned later that FBI agents had been spying for years on her father.

In April 1942, Yuri, her older brother Arthur, and her mother were taken to one of the assembly centers for Japanese Americans, set up hastily in fairgrounds and race tracks while relocation camps in remote areas of western states and Arkansas were being built. "My family was billeted in horse stalls at the Santa Anita [California] Racetrack," Yuri reported. "The smell of the manure made many Issei sick." But they and others did the best they could to make their small spaces livable, creating furniture out of boxes and making curtains "for privacy in the latrines."[15] Eventually, Yuri and her family were assigned to a concentration camp in Jerome, Arkansas. Nearby was Camp Shelby, Mississippi, where, ironically, many soldiers of Japanese descent were trained and became part of the 442nd Regimental Combat Battalion. During the war, the 442nd was the most highly decorated of any battalion for its size and length of service.

Yuri met and married one of the Camp Shelby soldiers, Bill Kochiyama, and after the war the couple moved to New York City, where they became involved in many civil rights efforts. They also were active in Japanese American Redress and Reparations Committees—efforts to win reparations to Japanese Americans for the losses they incurred while in concentration camps. Some Japanese Americans received payment for property that had been confiscated. In 1988, the U.S. government allocated twenty thousand dollars each to sixty thousand Japanese Americans.

Although no acts of espionage or sabotage by people of Japanese ancestry were ever found, President Franklin D. Roosevelt issued Executive Order 9066 that authorized the secretary of war to set up concentration camps (euphemistically called relocation centers) in remote areas of the United States. More than 120,000 men, women, and children of Japanese descent (among them 70,000 American citizens) were forced from their homes and businesses, losing an estimated four billion dollars in property and income. They were tagged like baggage and sent to camps surrounded by barbed wire and guarded by the military. After World War II, the U.S. government made some payment to American Japanese who lost property, but many claims were denied on the grounds that the military had acted out of necessity, which was later proven false.

Decades later, the U.S. Congress passed the Civil Liberties Act of 1988, which President Ronald Reagan signed. The act included an apology for a "grave injustice" done to Japanese Americans and provided for a token payment of twenty thousand dollars each to more than sixty thousand survivors of the relocation camps.

Bigotry and Intolerance Worldwide

Historians have filled countless pages with stories about nativism, bigotry, and intolerance in the United States, but these traits have been as strong or stronger in other countries. A notorious example is the view held by German Nazis during the 1930s and 1940s, the time of World War II. Nazi leader Adolf Hitler claimed Aryans (meaning pureblooded gentile Germans) were the superior race and that

The National Holocaust Museum

At the National Holocaust Museum in Washington, D.C., visitors receive four-page identification cards that tell brief stories of Holocaust survivors. One of those cards was about teenager Jacob Wasserman who was born in Krakow, Poland, in 1926. According to his story, "Jacob was the eldest of three sons born to religious Jewish parents in the city of Krakow. His father was a flour merchant. The Wassermans spent summer vacations near Proszowice at a farm owned by their grandfather, who also ran a flour mill." The story continues in Jacob's words:

1933–39: In March 1939, at the age of 13, I celebrated my bar mitzvah. That summer we vacationed as usual at my grandfather's farm. We returned to a nightmare. Krakow had been occupied by the Germans on September 6. Jews were not allowed to walk on the sidewalks, to ride streetcars, or even to own radios. We were even afraid to walk in the streets because Jews were often kidnapped and beaten.

1940–45: In 1940, we retreated to the farm. Early one Saturday, the Jews in the area were rounded up. We were being marched into Proszowice when a Polish policeman—two dead bodies next to him—motioned to me demanding why I hadn't greeted him "Good morning." As I came closer he loaded his gun and pointed it at me. But as I passed, he bashed me with the barrel, smashing my nose and jaw. I broke away and lost myself in the column; the policeman shot someone else instead. Four days later my father and I were deported to the Prokocim camp.[16]

During most of the war Jacob was detained in labor camps. But he eventually was freed, and in 1948 he settled in Israel.

There are a total of 598 stories on the *Holocaust Encyclopedia* website at www.ushmm.org/wlc/en/a2z.php?type=idcard.

the purity of the German blood had to be protected from Jews, whom Hitler labeled as an inferior race although biologically there is no such thing as a Jewish race. People of many diverse national groups practice the religion and are part of the culture of Judaism.

As is well known, many Germans accepted Hitler's bigotry and hatred and the result was the Holocaust, one of the most horrifying mass murders in recent history—the killing of six million Jews and others who were considered inferior such as Roma (or gypsies in English), the mentally retarded, and people who defied the Nazis in Germany and Nazi-occupied nations.

Bigotry and intolerance have brought misery and death to millions of other people around the world. Just a few examples:

- During World War I (1915–1918), Turks, who were primarily Muslims, carried out a planned and sustained attack against the people of Armenia, a part of the vast Ottoman Empire that stretched from the Middle East to northern Africa to southern and eastern Europe. Thousands of Christian Armenians were systematically killed or were sent to the desert, where they died of starvation or dehydration. Although peace prevailed for a time after World War I, between 1920 and 1923, Armenians were once again massacred or forcefully removed from their lands.

A sculpture at the Holocaust museum in Jerusalem.

- In Cambodia between 1975 and 1979, the Khmer Rouge Communist Party under the rule of Pol Pot and his associates carried out a systematic extermination of urban citizens, intellectuals, and minority individuals. Communists executed or starved to death nearly two million Cambodians in their effort to create an "ideal" agrarian society.
- During the 1990s, Bosnia Herzegovina, Serbian, and Yugoslavian President Slobodan Milosevic and other political leaders initiated a plan for "ethnic cleansing." The plan called for forcefully relocating non-Serbs who were primarily Roman Catholic Croats and Muslims. "As a precursor to this policy, non-Serbs were identified as traitors, and a massive propaganda campaign started. . . . Ethnic cleansing evolved into religious genocide, with systematic destruction of libraries and mosques, mass, systematic rape of women, and mass killing of non-Serbs," reported ReligiousTolerance.org.[17]

In China, Russia, Rwanda, and other parts of the world similar atrocities have been committed either as a form of ethnic cleansing or as acts of hateful intolerance.

Notes

1. Kiri Davis, director, *A Girl Like Me*, Reel Works Teen Filmmaking, n.d., www.understand ingrace.org/lived/video/index.html (accessed February 10, 2012).
2. Davis, *A Girl Like Me*.
3. Gordon W. Allport, *The Nature of Prejudice*, 10th ed. (Reading, MA: Addison-Wesley Publishing Company, 1979), 13.
4. American Anthropological Association, "Statement on 'Race,'" May 17, 1998, www.aaanet .org/stmts/racepp.htm (February 9, 2012).
5. E. O. Wilson, "Biologist E. O. Wilson on Why Humans, Like Ants, Need a Tribe," *Daily Beast*, April 1, 2012, www.thedailybeast.com/newsweek/2012/04/01/biologist-e-o-wilson-on -why-humans-like-ants-need-a-tribe.print.html (accessed April 14, 2012).
6. Wilson, "Biologist E. O. Wilson on Why Humans, Like Ants, Need a Tribe."
7. Kathlyn Gay, *I Am Who I Am: Speaking Out about Multiracial Identity* (New York: Franklin Watts, 1995), 57.
8. Frank M. Snowden Jr., *Before Color Prejudice: The Ancient View of Blacks* (Cambridge, MA: Harvard University Press, 1983), 108.
9. David E. Stannard, *American Holocaust: Columbus and the Conquest of the New World* (New York: Oxford University Press, 1992), 180.
10. Colin Nickerson and Junko Fujita, "In Japan, 'Different' Is Dangerous," *Boston Globe*, January 24, 1993, National/Foreign section, 1.
11. John Jay, "The Federalist No. 2 Concerning Dangers from Foreign Force and Influence," *Independent Journal*, October 31, 1787, www.constitution.org/fed/federa02.htm (accessed December 6, 2012).

12. Frank Soulé, John H. Gihon, MD, and James Nisbet. *The Annals of San Francisco*, 1854, www.sfgenealogy.com/sf/history/hbann2-20.htm (accessed February 11, 2012).

13. *Personal Justice Denied: Report of the Commission on Wartime Relocation and Internment of Civilians*, December 1982, last modified January 8, 2007, chapter 2, www.nps.gov/history/history/online_books/personal_justice_denied/chap2.htm.

14. Yuri Kochiyama, *Passing It On* (Los Angeles: UCLA Asian American Studies Center Press, 2004), xxiii.

15. Kochiyama, *Passing It On*, 12.

16. United States Holocaust Memorial Museum, "Identification Card," card #7472 in the author's collection. Also see United States Holocaust Memorial Museum, "The Holocaust," *Holocaust Encyclopedia*, www.ushmm.org/wlc/en/?ModuleId=10005143 (accessed February 19, 2012).

17. B. A. Robinson, "Mass Crimes against Humanity and Genocides," ReligiousTolerance.org, last updated November 15, 2009, www.religioustolerance.org/genocide4.htm (accessed February 13, 2012).

3

RELIGIOUS BIGOTRY

···

"Once I learned the basics of Wicca it felt right to me. I felt at peace.
I realized that Wicca wasn't evil and that it was meant for me to learn more about it.
My parents wouldn't allow that to happen. They told me that I had to go to
Church that I was wrong and evil. My older sister even told me that I was going
to go to Hell."—Jasmine Hodges, a high school senior, writing in Teen Ink
about how she found Wicca[1]

The Canadian-based ReligiousTolerance.org has introduced a type of bigotry that it calls *religism*, defined as "the expression of fear towards, hatred towards, or discrimination against, persons of a specific religion affiliation, usually a minority faith." On its website, the organization states,

> Unfortunately, the English language does not have a widely accepted word to refer to bigotry based on religion. Yet, in our opinion, religious bigotry is the single most important impediment to world peace. If the human race is wiped off the face of the earth later in this century, the root cause will probably be religious bigotry triggering World War III. The most common form of religism in North America is in the form of discrimination against non-Christians, up to and including the promotion of genocide against them.

Most religious groups believe that their faith is the only "true" religion, and this belief sometimes results in discrimination, harassment, and physical attacks against people of another faith. In fact, ReligiousTolerance.org notes, "Religious bigotry may well have been the most common form of bigotry for much of Europe's history. Most of us are familiar with the persecution of Christians in ancient Rome, in which they were fed to the lions in the Coliseum and even blamed for the burning of Rome. During the Middle Ages the Jews were persecuted to no end, not just because they were another ethnic group, but another religion as well."[2]

Religious bigotry, of course, was not confined to ancient times and the Middle Ages. It was an inherent part of the lives of explorers and settlers who traveled from the Old World to the New World of the Americas during the 1600s. And, in fact, forms of religious bigotry are evident in many areas of U.S. society today, as teenager Jessica Ahlquist can tell you.

Jessica experienced religious bigotry except that it was because she did not believe in an organized faith. She is an atheist and declares she has been a nonbeliever since she was ten years old. As she told a *New York Times* reporter, "I had always been told that if you pray, God will always be there when you need him," she said. "And it didn't happen for me, and I doubted it had happened for anybody else. So yeah, I think that was just like the last step, and after that I just really didn't believe any of it."[3] Jessica makes no secret of her nonbelief, which has brought her much criticism and even death threats from townspeople in Cranston, Rhode Island.

It all started in 2010 when Jessica complained to Cranston High School West officials about a prayer banner on the wall of the auditorium. The banner had been there "since 1963, when a seventh grader wrote it as a sort of moral guide and that year's graduating class presented it as a gift. It was a year after a landmark Supreme Court ruling barring organized prayer in public schools," according to *New York Times* reporter Abby Goodnough.

The eight-foot high banner is titled *School Prayer* and begins with these words in all capital letters:

OUR HEAVENLY FATHER.
GRANT US EACH DAY THE DESIRE TO DO OUR BEST, TO GROW MENTALLY AND MORALLY AS WELL AS PHYSICALLY, TO BE KIND AND HELPFUL. . . .

It ends with

HELP US ALWAYS TO CONDUCT OURSELVES SO AS TO BRING CREDIT TO CRANSTON HIGH SCHOOL WEST.
AMEN[4]

High school officials did nothing about the banner. However, an anonymous parent contacted the American Civil Liberties Union (ACLU). The ACLU filed a lawsuit with Jessica as a plaintiff against the school district.

In January 2012, "A federal judge ruled . . . that the prayer's presence at Cranston High School West was unconstitutional, concluding that it violated the principle of government neutrality in religion." The judge ordered the banner's removal. Since that ruling, townspeople and politicians have called for an appeal

Bans on Religious Groups in New York City's Public Schools

Some call a ban on religious groups in New York City's public schools "egregious religious bigotry." Others say religious groups should not be allowed to worship in public school buildings that are supported by taxpayer funds. Since the mid-1990s, New York City congregations that have lost their churches have rented spaces in public schools when students are not in class. Mayor Michael Bloomberg and the city's education department declared religious services in public schools violated the separation of church and state, and in February 2012, they banned religious groups from using vacant public schools, although other community groups have had access to campuses for their activities.

In 1995, a Bronx church sued the city, claiming that the ban violated the First Amendment, which allows for the free exercise of religion. A court temporarily blocked the ban but a higher court upheld it. Mayor Bloomberg has been adamant about keeping church and state separate. At a press conference in mid-February 2012, he said, "I've always thought that one of the great things about America is that we keep a separation between church and state and the more clear that separation is, the more those people who want to be able to practice their religion will have the opportunity to do so."[5] In a radio address, he said, "Separation of church and state are [*sic*] one of the basics of our country. . . . The more religious you are the more you should want to keep the separation, because someday the religion that the state picks as the 'state religion' might not be yours. The way to solve that is to not have a state religion."[6] However, in late June 2012, a federal judge ruled that banning religious groups from using schools outside regular school hours, while allowing other groups to use public schools, violates the First Amendment clause. The city immediately planned to appeal the decision.

and have publicly condemned Jessica, calling her "evil" and "an idiot."[7] At times she had to have a police escort to school. When Jessica's supporters tried to send her flowers, florists refused to deliver them.

Nevertheless, she has hundreds of friends and defenders on Facebook and Twitter. One supporter, Hemant Mehta, wrote, "The way she has handled herself throughout this whole ordeal is admirable far beyond anything most people would expect from a high school student."[8] Mehta conducted a scholarship drive and by the end of February 2012, the last day of his drive, the fund totaled more than $48,000. The Rhode Island chapter of the American Humanist Association, a national organization for atheists, also collected scholarship donations and in late March 2012, the association gave Jessica a check for $62,618.

Another highly controversial religious issue erupted in 2012 when the Obama administration issued a policy requiring employers in religious institutions to provide birth-control insurance coverage for employees. Catholics and other religious groups who believe contraception is contradictory to their beliefs were outraged. President Obama offered a compromise: Religious institutions would not have to pay the costs of providing birth control for employees. Rather the costs would be covered by insurance companies. But that did not satisfy religious leaders or those who support them, such as the bombastic radio talk show personality Rush Limbaugh.

For days Limbaugh, who claims to be a Methodist but does not attend church, ranted about the contraceptive policy and was especially irate when Sandra Fluke, a law student at Georgetown University, testified before a congressional committee on February 23, 2012. A Jesuit school, Georgetown does not cover contraception in its health-care insurance. Fluke was representing Law Students for Reproductive Justice and said in part, "When I look around my campus, I see the faces of the women affected by this lack of contraceptive coverage." She noted that on a daily basis she has heard from women who have "suffered financially and emotionally and medically because of the lack of coverage." She pointed out, "Without insurance coverage, contraception can cost a woman over $3,000 during law school. For a lot of students who, like me, are on public interest scholarships, that's practically an entire summer's salary." In her testimony, Fluke explained how women who have ovarian cysts use birth control prescriptions to stop cyst growths. Other health problems also are treated with contraceptive pills, she noted.[9]

Limbaugh's reaction was ugly bigotry. In his words, which were broadcast repeatedly on news shows,

> What does it say about the college co-ed Fluke who goes before a congressional committee and essentially says that she must be paid to have sex? What does that make her? It makes her a slut, right? It makes her a prosti-

What They Said. What Do You Think?

"I'm telling you that everybody who runs CNN is a lot like [*The Daily Show* host Jon] Stewart, and a lot of people who run all the other networks are a lot like Stewart, and to imply that somehow they—the people in this country who are Jewish—are an oppressed minority? *Yeah* [sarcastically]."—Rick Sanchez talking to Pete Dominick on a radio show in October 2010

"The bigotry against pro-life people is I think way more than the bigotry against gay people. Particularly in the media because the media supports gay people in this country."—Bill O'Reilly on his show February 7, 2012

"Mormonism was created by a guy in upstate New York in 1830 when he got caught having sex with the maid and explained to his wife that God told him to do it. Forty-eight wives later, Joseph Smith's lifestyle was completely sanctified in the religion he invented to go with it. Which Mitt Romney [Republican presidential candidate] says he believes."—Lawrence O'Donnell on his show April 4, 2012

"There's a lot more anti-Christian bigotry today than there is concerning the other side. And none of it gets covered by the news media."—former U.S. House of Representative Speaker Newt Gingrich during a Republican debate on January 7, 2012

"In the name of equality, the [U.S.] Supreme Court has declared the practice of homosexuality to be a constitutional right. . . . Although gay marriage has been rejected in 31 states in referenda, judges continue to declare that such unions be treated as marriages. An idea of equality rejected democratically by voters is being imposed dictatorially. In December 2010, a repudiated liberal Congress imposed its San Francisco values on the Armed Forces, by ordering homosexuals admitted to all branches of the service."—from political analyst Pat Buchanan's book *Suicide of a Superpower: Will America Survive to 2025?* (2011), p. 211

Are *any* of the preceding comments expressions of *religious* bigotry? What do you think?

tute. She wants to be paid to have sex. She's having so much sex she can't afford the contraception. She wants you and me and the taxpayers to pay her to have sex. What does that make us? We're the pimps.

As if that was not enough he charged: "If we're going to have to pay for this, then we want something in return, Ms. Fluke. And that would be the videos of all this sex posted online so we can see what we're getting for our money."[10]

The public outrage against Limbaugh was swift and furious. By early March 2012, dozens of companies that had advertised on Limbaugh's show dropped their commercials, and several radio stations declared they would not broadcast the show. Chris Leonard, president and general manager of New West Broadcasting in Hilo, Hawaii, said in a statement, "We are strong believers in the first amendment and have recognized Mr. Limbaugh's right to express opinions that often times differ from our own, but it has never been our goal to allow our station to be used for personal attacks and intolerance. The most recent incident has crossed a line of decency and a standard that we expect of programming on KPUA."[11] After much pressure from the public, politicians, advertisers, and even faculty members and the president of Georgetown University, Limbaugh publicly apologized to Sandra Fluke. Petitions to remove Limbaugh from the air waves continued for months. Yet, Limbaugh prevails, and those who follow his program are still loyal listeners.

A Long History of American Religious Bigotry

The religious bigotry of current times is not a new development. Early settlers in North America sought religious liberty, but they did not allow it for all. In Virginia, the first English colony, the founders set up the official Anglican Church patterned after the Church of England. The Virginia founders expected to develop a replica of a British community, including an established government-supported church. All colonists regardless of their religious beliefs were taxed to pay for the building and maintenance of the Anglican Church, which later became known as the Episcopal Church. Laws also mandated that people attend church, and there were harsh penalties for those who did not abide by the church teaching.

Some British settlers in North America completely separated themselves from the Church of England. These dissenters, known as Pilgrims, founded the Plymouth colony in Massachusetts. They hoped to be free of a state-mandated church.

Another well-known group of British dissenters, the Puritans, founded the Massachusetts Bay Colony, which they expected to be a "heavenly city" governed by biblical codes. Rules covered not only church attendance but also clothing, the conduct of business, the education of children, and permissible types of recre-

The Salem Witch Trials

In January 1692, Salem Village (present-day Danvers, Massachusetts) in the Massachusetts Bay Colony was the scene of mass hysteria. Three young girls, nine-year-old Elizabeth Parris, daughter of a minister; her cousin Abigail Williams, age eleven; and eleven-year-old Ann Putnam from another family were exhibiting strange behavior, screaming, making odd sounds, throwing things, and writhing around. Villagers believed that Satan was at work and that witches, possessed with the devil, had cast spells on the girls. At the time, engaging in witchcraft was a felony punishable by death.

Villagers began praying and fasting in order to rid their community of Satan's presence. And the girls were questioned repeatedly to reveal the names of witches who controlled them. Eventually the girls named three women: an impoverished elderly woman, a homeless woman, and Tituba, a slave in the Parris family household. The three women were questioned by a judge for several days. Tituba was the only one who confessed. According to a historical account by Jess Blumberg in *Smithsonian.com*, Tituba said, "The Devil came to me and bid me serve him." She described elaborate images of black dogs, red cats, yellow birds, and a "black man" who wanted her to sign his book. She admitted that she signed the book and said there were several other witches looking to destroy the Puritans. All three women were put in jail.[12]

Along with the three jailed women, dozens more, including a four-year-old girl, were questioned and accused of witchcraft. A special court was established to hear the cases of the alleged witches, totaling more than two hundred people. From June through September 1692, nineteen people were convicted and hanged on what became known as Gallows Hill for the crime of witchcraft. A seventy-one-year-old man who refused to confess to witchcraft was tortured; he was pressed to death with heavy stones.

Cotton Mather, an influential Puritan minister, wrote to the Massachusetts governor, William Phipps, urging him to stop the trials. By the spring of 1693, the governor finally heeded Mather's plea. Blumberg notes in *Smithsonian*, "On

January 14, 1697, the General Court ordered a day of fasting and soul-searching for the tragedy of Salem. In 1702, the court declared the trials unlawful. And in 1711, the colony passed a bill restoring the rights and good names of those accused and granted £600 [about $960] restitution to their heirs. However, it was not until 1957—more than 250 years later—that Massachusetts formally apologized for the events of 1692."[13]

ation. Only members of what became the Congregational Church, the established religion, were allowed to vote, and membership was limited to those whose beliefs and lifestyles conformed to church doctrine. The leaders of the Massachusetts Bay Colony strictly enforced church rules and harassed and drove out Catholics and members of such Protestant groups as Baptists and Quakers. In short, the Puritans were religious bigots—intolerant of those who did not conform to their beliefs.

Massachusetts was not alone in its religious intolerance. Except for Rhode Island, Pennsylvania, and Delaware, the rest of the colonies, whether settled by the British, Dutch, or others, established state churches. Whatever the established church, it protected the interests of the majority, while oppressing those dissenters who might disrupt the social order.

As an increasing number of settlers with varying backgrounds arrived in North America, conditions slowly changed. For one thing, many more people who opposed the idea of an established church populated the land.

Not long before declaring independence, each of the colonies that would soon be states, developed a written constitution, a legal framework for the way each government would function. In Virginia, one of the first laws abolished the mandate for church attendance and repealed punishments for those people whose religious practices differed from the established religion.

When the U.S. Constitution was adopted in 1789, it included only a brief statement about religion, part of which said "no religious Test shall ever be required as a Qualification to any Office or public Trust under the United States." That left many Americans concerned because the Constitution did not specifically assure civil and religious liberties for the people. Eventually the Constitution was amended. The First Amendment of the Constitution begins with the sentence, "Congress shall make no laws respecting the establishment of religion, or prohibiting the free exercise thereof; or abridging the freedom of speech, or of the press; or the right of the people peacefully to assemble." Over the years, when Americans have exercised their First Amendment rights, their actions sometimes have sparked heated debates, especially when religious beliefs or views are the basis for arguments.

Consider some religious groups such as Jehovah's Witnesses, some Mennonites, and others who believe that pledging allegiance to any country's flag is an offense against biblical laws. This belief was in direct conflict with state laws that required American schoolchildren to take part in a ceremony pledging allegiance to the U.S. flag. Children who did not participate could be expelled from school, and in a few states their parents could be charged with a criminal offense.

In 1935, seventh grader Lillian Gobitas and her brother, fifth grader William, members of Jehovah's Witnesses in Minersville, Pennsylvania, refused to salute the U.S. flag in their public school classroom. Lillian recalled that because of her action, "everyone was staring at me" but she "felt elated," because it was against her religious beliefs to salute any flag.[14] The two children were expelled from the school. Their father, Walter Gobitas, challenged the mandatory flag salute and pledge, arguing in a lawsuit that the First Amendment protected his children's right to refuse to take part in the flag ceremony. Although Gobitas won several court decisions, in 1940 the case known as *Minersville School District v. Gobitis* (the Gobitas name was misspelled) went to the U.S. Supreme Court, which upheld the law, declaring that the ceremony promoted unity and national security.

The Gobitas case created great controversy. At the time, the United States was on the verge of war and some Americans thought the Gobitas family and other Jehovah's Witnesses were disloyal and unpatriotic. Across the United States, mobs attacked Jehovah's Witnesses and set meeting places on fire. At the same time, Americans who felt that First Amendment rights had been violated began to protest the Court's decision. Religious leaders, legal experts, and others wrote articles and spoke out in favor of the Witnesses' right to act according to their beliefs. In 1943, the Supreme Court accepted another flag salute case involving Jehovah's Witnesses, *West Virginia State Board of Education v. Barnette*, and the Court reversed its earlier ruling.

Another religious group that has had conflicts with state laws is the Amish, known as plain people, who are descendants of sixteenth-century Swiss Anabaptists. The Old Order Amish are the most conservative of the Anabaptists, who also include Brethren, Hutterites, and Mennonites. Since their arrival in North America centuries ago, the Amish have maintained a simple lifestyle on family farms, wearing plain clothing and doing without electricity, modern transportation, farm equipment, and technology.

The Amish believe their children should attend school only through the eighth grade and should not have to abide by state laws requiring compulsory education until the age of sixteen. Amish teenagers are expected to work on the family farm or in a family business, making furniture or buggies or operating a fabric shop. "Through the 1940s and 1950s, Amish parents were taken to court, fined, even sent to jail for refusing to permit their children to attend schools past the age of fourteen or for sending them to Amish-run schools whose teachers were not state-certified and whose educational and safety standards were deemed inadequate," wrote author Tom Shachtman in his book *Rumspringa: To Be or Not to Be Amish.*[15]

Over the years, several states have tried to force Amish youth to attend public schools until they reached the age of sixteen. Some of the most controversial actions took place in Iowa in 1965. Against the advice of the Iowa attorney general, state truant officers went into an Amish school, planning to force the children to take a school bus to a public school. But the press was on the scene when the truant officers arrived. After the story was published, people across the nation criticized the actions of the Iowa school officials. Although the Iowa governor tried to mediate and said he was willing to bend the laws, it was not until 1967 that the Iowa legislature changed its school law to allow exemptions because of religious beliefs.

A similar situation existed in Wisconsin during the 1970s. An Amish family refused to obey compulsory education laws, and the case went to the U.S. Supreme Court. The Court ruled that compulsory education jeopardized the freedom of the Amish to live by their religious beliefs.

Intolerance of Conscientious Objectors

In the past, the U.S. government has required a draft, or compulsory military service for young men (women have been exempt). Under the U.S. Selective Service System, which is responsible for inducting draftees, millions of young men have served in World Wars I and II, in the Korean War during the 1950s, and in the war in Vietnam during the 1960s and 1970s. In 1973, as U.S. troops in Vietnam were reduced, military service became voluntary. Currently, young men are not drafted, but those between the ages of eighteen and twenty-five are required to register with the U.S. Selective Service System in case conscription (the draft) becomes a necessity.

During every war, there have been men strongly opposed to armed conflict and have refused to fight on the basis of religious grounds or strongly held ethical, humanitarian, and philosophical principles. They have applied for conscientious objector (CO) status, which is a legal exemption that allows people to perform noncombat service in hospitals, forestry, and highway departments. COs also have served as clerks and farmhands. Even if young men are not subject to a draft today, they can apply for CO status when they register with the Selective Service.

However, COs have faced formidable problems. At the very least, some Americans have accused COs of being cowards and disloyal to their country. In some cases, COs have been jailed and tortured. In other instances, COs have been deprived of their civil rights.

Perhaps there is no more widely publicized CO claim than that of Muhammad Ali, former heavyweight boxing champion, whose case is still discussed today. In 1965, Ali became a member and minister of the Nation of Islam (NOI), a black religious group that some people consider controversial. In 1968 during the Vietnam War, Ali went before the draft board in Houston, Texas, and refused to be inducted into the armed forces, resisting on religious grounds. Many Americans were incensed, refusing to believe that Ali was a minister or part of a religious group.

The U.S. Department of Justice claimed that Ali simply belonged to a political organization. Ali was arrested, convicted of draft evasion, and sentenced to prison. He was also stripped of the title he had won as boxing champion of the world. He appealed his conviction and while the appeal process took place, he toured the country. The U.S. Supreme Court heard Ali's case in 1971 and found Ali's CO status valid. The Court overruled his draft-evasion conviction. When Ali talked to a sports reporter about his refusal to take up arms, he told his side of the story:

> In Houston, when I was asked to stand up and be sworn into the service, I thought about . . . all the lynching, raping and killing [black people had] suffered and there was an Army fellow my age acting like god and telling me to go to Viet Nam and fight Asians who'd never called me Nigger, had never lynched me, had never put dogs on me. . . . I said to myself, this guy in the Army suit ain't God—so when he asked me to step forward I just stayed there. . . . I knew the war was wrong, it was against my religious beliefs, and I was willing to go to jail for those beliefs.[16]

Islamaphobia

Since the September 11, 2001, attacks on the United States, there have been escalating tensions surrounding Islam in America. For example, there have been protests against a mosque near "ground zero," the site where New York City's World Trade Center, which was destroyed by terrorists, once stood. In Florida, a pastor threatened to burn the Quran in public. In September 2010, a twenty-one-year-old college student pointed out how others' fear of Islam (Islamaphobia) has affected him. He expressed his anonymous opinion on the website of Our American Generation (OAG), an organization established in Seattle, Washington, with an Internet site that presents ways youth can create social justice. He wrote about a New York student, twenty-one-year-old Michael Enright, who in August 2010 stabbed a Bangladesh cab driver after learning he was Muslim. By stating greetings in Arabic and asking friendly questions, Michael Enright earned [the cab driver] Ahmed Sharif's trust before slashing him with a leatherman in the throat, lip, and arm. This horrifying event changed one thing for me: as an Arabic learner, I usually enjoyed talking with cab drivers about whether they were from an Arabic-speaking country, or whether they were Muslim. Now, I feel that asking such questions could make taxi drivers suspicious or nervous, and that is an uncomfortable feeling. Thanks to this one individual who I have no connection with, other than the fact that I happen to be a 21 year old college student, I have to be more careful about innocent actions, like asking a cab driver where he is from.[17]

In the town of Murfreesboro, Tennessee, some residents in 2010 and 2011 protested the building of a mosque in their town, claiming that Islam was not a real religion. The protesters also argued that Muslims planned to overthrow the U.S. Constitution and replace it with Islamic law. They posted signs saying, "Muslims Not Welcome." The city approved construction of the mosque, but vandals and an arsonist damaged the building. In addition, the congregation had to get a permit to occupy the mosque. Finally, in July 2012, a federal judge ordered that the Islamic Center of Murfreesboro be given a permit, and Muslims were able to worship in their building.

Then there is the story of Shoshana Hebshi, who describes herself as "a half-Arab, half-Jewish" housewife living in Ohio. She was on her way home, flying from Denver, Colorado, to Detroit, Michigan, and driving the rest of the way to Ohio. It was September 11, 2011, and she (as well as two Indian men) was pulled off a plane in Detroit, Michigan. As she explained on her blog, "Someone on the plane had reported that the three of us in row 12 were conducting suspicious activity. What is the likelihood that two Indian men who didn't know each other and a dark-skinned woman of Arab/Jewish heritage would be on the same flight from Denver to Detroit? Was that suspicion enough? Even considering that we didn't say a word to each other until it became clear there were cops following our plane?" Hebshi was handcuffed, strip searched, locked in a cell, and interrogated for hours. As she noted,

When the Patriot Act was passed after 9/11 and Arabs and Arab-looking people were being harassed all over the country, my Saudi Arabian dad became nervous. A bit of a conspiracy theorist at heart, he knew the government was watching him and at any time could come and take him away. It was happening all over. Men were being taken on suspicion of terrorist activities and held and questioned—sometimes abused—for long periods of time. Our country had a civil rights issue on its hands. And, in the name of patriotism we lost a lot of our liberty, especially those who look like me. . . .

I believe in national security, but I also believe in peace and justice. I believe in tolerance, acceptance and trying—as hard as it sometimes may be—not to judge a person by the color of their skin or the way they dress.[18]

Yet judging people by their religious dress and practices continues and it can turn deadly, as it did on Sunday, August 5, 2012. That morning at a Sikh *gurdwara*, or temple, in the Milwaukee suburb of Oak Creek, Wisconsin, Wade Michael Page, a neo-Nazi and singer with a white-power band, shot and killed six members of the temple and injured three (some reports say four) others. It is not unusual for Sikhs—especially men—to be targeted by hate-group members. As part of their religious practices Sikh men wear a turban and grow a beard and frequently are mistaken for Muslims or Hindus. The turban has been part of the Sikh tradition ever since the founding of the religion in the Punjab region of India, now Pakistan, during the late fifteenth century.

During Page's shooting spree, police quickly responded to 911 calls from worshippers hiding in the temple. Initial reports said that Page was killed by police officers who shot Page in the stomach. But an agent in the Federal Bureau of Investigation's Milwaukee office reported that after being wounded, Page died by shooting himself in the head.

In 2012 a *New York Times* report noted, "Intolerance seems to be part of the message sent to student-athletes on the sporting fields of Texas." An Islamic high school wanted to join the Texas Association of Private and Parochial Schools (known as Tapps) in order to compete in soccer games. In 2010 the school received a questionnaire that said in part, "It is our understanding that the Quran tells you not to mix with (and even eliminate) the infidels. Christians and Jews fall into that category. Why do you wish to join an organization whose membership is in disagreement with your religious beliefs?" The school answered the questionnaire but was denied membership. The *Times* also reported that Tapps "surveyed member schools about allowing in Islamic schools. Sixty-three percent of 83 respondents rejected Islamic schools for membership in 2010, according to school officials. The others said it was in Tapps's best interest to be open. Ten schools said they would quit Tapps if Islamic members were admitted."[19]

Intolerance and Bigotry against Jews

Louis Farrakhan, a black Muslim leader and head of the NOI for thirty years, often exhibits his religious intolerance in his oratory. In his speeches he has made "hateful statements targeting Jews, whites and homosexuals." Farrakhan has continually blamed all whites ("devils" he calls them) for problems blacks face, spouting a particular hatred for Jews, whom Farrakhan calls "bloodsuckers." According to the Anti-Defamation League,

> During his keynote address at the NOI's 2011 Saviours' Day convention in Rosemont, Illinois, Farrakhan blamed Jews for killing Jesus and accused Jews of controlling the U.S. government and banking industries. . . . In a 2010 lecture series that was rife with anti-Semitism and conspiracy theories, for example, Farrakhan downplayed historical Jewish suffering, accused Jews of world domination and promoted anti-Semitic charges of Jewish deicide [killing a deity]. He also repeated many of his past accusations about Jewish involvement in the transatlantic slave trade, Jewish exploitation of Black labor in the cotton trade, and Jewish control over government, finance and entertainment.[20]

Farrakhan is not alone in his anti-Jewish bigotry. Some examples: Nineteen-year-old Colin Andrew Ford of Norristown, Pennsylvania, spray-painted swastikas on a Jewish family's house in February 2011.[21] At the Florida National Cemetery near Bushnell, vandals knocked over thirteen headstones of Jewish veterans and their spouses. All of the grave markers were etched with the Star of David. The desecration has been called a hate crime.[22]

Religious Bigotry and Politics

During the 2012 U.S. presidential campaigns, religious bigotry was overt and covert in comments from candidates and their supporters and/or detractors. For example, one candidate, businessman Herman Cain, touted his Christianity and said he would not tolerate a Muslim in his administration. He also declared he would build an electrified fence on the border with Mexico, ostensibly to kill illegal immigrants. And at many rallies and talk shows, former speaker of the U.S. House of Representatives Newt Gingrich accused President Obama of "waging war on religion in America." Gingrich even offered to debate the president's religious bigotry.[23] Yet Obama is no religious bigot. He has consistently tried to encourage religious groups to work together.

In an October 2011 political gathering, Pastor Robert Jeffress of the First Baptist Church of Dallas, Texas, announced his support for Republican presidential candidate Texas governor Rick Perry, declaring, "Every true, born-again follower of Christ ought to embrace a Christian over a non-Christian." Jeffress went on to say that Republican candidate former Massachusetts governor Mitt Romney, who is a Mormon, is part of a "cult" and is not a Christian.[24]

Mormons and Fundamentalists

The Mormon Church was established in the early 1800s under the leadership of Joseph Smith, who called himself a prophet. He declared that he had received revelations from God, which he wrote down in the Book of Mormon, considered a supplement to the Protestant Bible.

While many Mormon beliefs are similar to traditional Christian concepts, Smith's claim that he received divine revelations was offensive if not heretical to many Americans. In addition, Smith advocated a strict patriarchal rule—men dominated women in family, religious, and civic matters. Mormon men also were expected to practice polygamy whenever possible, and that practice sparked antagonism in areas of the Midwest where Mormons lived. In fact, there were violent attacks against Mormons, and Smith and his brother were shot and killed.

In 1847, under the leadership of Brigham Young, a group of Mormons founded Salt Lake City in the Great Salt Lake Basin, a territory that became the state of Utah. Young attempted to set up a theocracy and continue the practice of polygamy, even though the practice was outlawed. Several years later, the polygamy issue was resolved when Utah territory applied for statehood in the 1890s. The territory was not allowed to join the union until it denounced polygamy, which leaders agreed to do.

In spite of the federal law banning polygamy, some LDS members broke away to found a sect called the Fundamentalist Church of Jesus Christ of Latter-Day Saints (FLDS), which continued plural marriages. A succession of men led the FLDS. In 2002, following the death of FLDS leader Rulon Jeffs, his son Warren Jeffs assumed leadership and he not only took possession of his father's wives but was also the sole person to assign wives for FLDS men. Jeffs dominated every aspect of members' lives. Movies, television, sports such as basketball and football were forbidden, and many male teenagers were excommunicated because they watched a movie or talked to a girl.

FLDS members lived on a compound, which included a temple and dozens of other buildings, south of San Angelo, Texas. In 2008, Texas authorities raided the compound after receiving a call on an abuse hotline. The call turned out to be a hoax, but police saw pregnant underage young girls (thirteen to fifteen years old) and later gathered evidence, including audio tapes and written records, that helped convict Jeffs of child rape, bigamy, and other crimes. Jeffs is serving a life sentence in prison, but he still issues orders from prison to the FLDS compound. News reporter Mike Watkiss has covered FLDS for twenty-five years and noted, "Anybody who thinks that Warren Jeffs' incarceration ended his rule in this community has no idea what they're talking about. He is in many ways more powerful because now he's martyred."[25]

After hearing Jeffress's words, former secretary of education William Bennett wrote,

I agree that there are serious theological differences between evangelical Christianity and Mormonism. But those should be settled in churches, in homes, and in religious gatherings, not in front of a national political event. Pastor Jeffress says his words were merely theological. He, pastor of a successful mega-church, should know full well the fine line between religion and politics. His words were clearly political, as evidenced by the damaging effect it had on the Republican presidential candidates and the national debate.[26]

Mormonism was a topic discussed repeatedly during the 2012 campaigns. But that was nothing new. Like the Baptist preacher Jeffress, many Americans long have believed that the Mormon Church (officially, the Church of Jesus Christ of Latter-Day Saints or the LDS Church) is a cult, which is false. Mormons also are accused of practicing polygamy—men having several wives—even though that practice was outlawed in 1862. A teenager in San Diego, California, put it succinctly in an article for *Teen Ink*, writing,

I am of a religion shunned constantly. I hear things like "You aren't Christian," "How [many] moms do you have?" or "You worship a dead man." These are all wrong, and we, the members of The Church of Jesus Christ of Latter Day Saints, are none of these. True, we practiced polygamy back in the 1800's, but it was repealed by our prophet only a few decades later. However, a group calling themselves "Fundamentalist Mormons" practice polygamy, but they are not, nor will they ever be, a faction of our church. . . . The Book of Mormon is another testament of Christ that we firmly

What Do You Think?

In March 2012, Florida's Governor Rick Scott signed a law that authorizes school boards to set policies for allowing students to pray or deliver "inspirational messages" at public school events. Florida legislators who supported the law believe it will help students be more tolerant of diverse religious beliefs.

But the other side noted that students who are not of the same faith as those leading a prayer or inspirational message could feel pressured to participate in a religious observance different from their own. Some religious leaders and organizations like the American Civil Liberties Union, Anti-Defamation League, and Americans United for Separation of Church and State contend that student prayers and inspirational messages could be the same as proselytizing and will encourage bigotry and intolerance.

What do you think?

believe in, thus we believe in Christ. How can we not be Christian when [we] pray in the name of Jesus Christ to God? How can anyone assume we do not believe in Christ when even our name has His name in this title.[27]

Other forms of religious bigotry have played out in the political arena as discussions and harangues focus on religious objections to abortion, gay rights, contraception, stem-cell research, prayer in public schools, holiday symbols on public property, creationism (versus evolution), immigration, climate change science, the death penalty, pledging allegiance to the U.S. flag, and other social and environmental issues.

Notes

1. Jasmine Hodges, "How I Found Wicca," *Teen Ink*, n.d., www.teenink.com/opinion/spirituality_religion/article/145060/How-I-found-Wicca/ (accessed June 9, 2012).
2. Ontario Consultants on Religious Tolerance, "A New English Word: 'Religism,' Which Means Bigotry Based on Religious Belief," ReligiousTolerance.org, n.d., www.religioustolerance.org/religism.htm (accessed February 21, 2012).

3. Abby Goodnough, "Student Faces Town's Wrath in Protest against a Prayer," *New York Times*, January 26, 2012, www.nytimes.com/2012/01/27/us/rhode-island-city-enraged-over -school-prayer-lawsuit.html (accessed June 30, 2012).

4. Bill Tomison, "Prayer Banner Controversy," *WPRI.com*, March 26, 2012, www.wpri .com/dpp/news/local_news/west_bay/providence-prayer-banner-critic-jessica-ahlquist-gets -humanist-scholarship (accessed August 23, 2012).

5. Jessica Schultz, "Bloomberg's School Worship Ban: Mayor Says 'Separation of Church and State,'" *International Business Times*, February 14, 2012, newyork.ibtimes.com/articles/ 298284/20120214/bloomberg-s-school-worship-ban-mayor-separation.htm (accessed March 4, 2012).

6. Michael Muskal, "Use New York Schools for Church? One Battle in an Ongoing Fight," *Los Angeles Times*, February 17, 2012, www.latimes.com/news/nation/nationnow/la-na-nn -church-state-battles20120217,0,5977629.story (accessed March 4, 2012).

7. Goodnough, "Student Faces Town's Wrath."

8. Rene Lynch, "Prayer Banner: Atheist Teen Speaks Out, Lands $44,000 Scholarship," *Los Angeles Times*, February 22, 2012, latimes.com/news/nation/nationnow/la-nn-na-jessica -ahlquist-atheist-teen-wins-40000-scholarship-20120222,0,6201324.story (accessed February 22, 2012).

9. Sandra Fluke, statement before congressional committee, February 23, 2012, abcnews. go.com/images/Politics/statement-Congress-letterhead-2nd%20hearing.pdf (accessed March 4, 2012).

10. Jack Mirkinson, "Rush Limbaugh: Sandra Fluke, Woman Denied Right to Speak at Contraception Hearing, a 'Slut,'" *Huffington Post*, February 29, 2012, www.huffingtonpost .com/2012/02/29/rush-limbaugh-sandra-fluke-slut_n_1311640.html (accessed December 7, 2012). See also note 11.

11. CNN Political Unit, "Stations, Advertisers Drop Limbaugh," *PoliticalTicker* (blog), political-ticker.blogs.cnn.com/2012/03/06/more-limbaugh-stations-advertisers-jump-ship/?hpt=hp _t3 (accessed March 6, 2012).

12. Jess Blumberg, "A Brief History of the Salem Witch Trials," *Smithsonian.com*, October 24, 2007, www.smithsonianmag.com/history-archaeology/brief-salem.html (accessed February 25, 2012).

13. Blumberg, "A Brief History."

14. Shawn Francis Peters, *Judging Jehovah's Witnesses: Religious Persecution and the Dawn of the Rights Revolution* (Lawrence: University Press of Kansas, 2000), 28.

15. Tom Shachtman, *Rumspringa: To Be or Not to Be Amish* (New York: North Point Press/Farrar, Straus, and Giroux, 2006), 102.

16. John D. McCallum, *The Encyclopedia of World Boxing Champions* (Radnor, PA: Chilton Book Company, 1975), 73.

17. Anonymous, "The Ground Zero Mosque and Islamaphobia in America," *OAG* (blog), September 11, 2010, oag.org/the-ground-zero-mosque-and-islamophobia-in-america/ (accessed February 28, 2012).

18. Shoshana Hebshi, "Some Real Shock and Awe: Racially Profiled and Cuffed in Detroit," *Stories from the Heartland* (blog), September 12, 2011, shebshi.wordpress.com/2011/09/12/ some-real-shock-and-awe-racially-profiled-and-cuffed-in-detroit/ (accessed February 21, 2012).

19. Editorial, "Bigotry on the Playing Field," *New York Times*, March 11, 2012, www.nytimes .com/2012/03/12/opinion/bigotry-on-the-playing-field.html?_r=1 (accessed March 12, 2012).

20. Anti-Defamation League, "Farrakhan in His Own Words," updated August 13, 2011, www .adl.org/special_reports/farrakhan_own_words2/farrakhan_own_words.asp (accessed January 23, 2012).

21. "For the Record," *Intelligence Report* (Montgomery, AL: Southern Poverty Law Center, Winter 2011), 48.

22. Tony Marrero, "Vandals Target Graves of Jewish Veterans, Spouses," *Tampa Bay Times*, March 8, 2012, 3.

23. See www.youtube.com/watch?v=wXyEum9wDM0 (accessed December 7, 2012).

24. William Bennett, "Don't Judge Candidates by Their Faith," *CNN*, October 11, 2011, www .cnn.com/2011/10/11/opinion/bennett-jeffress-mormon-comments/index.html (accessed March 1, 2012).

25. Muriel Pearson and Joseph Diaz, "Jailed Polygamist Leader Warren Jeffs Issues Hundreds of Orders from Prison," *ABC News*, November 21, 2012, abcnews.go.com/US/jailed -polygamist-leader-warren-jeffs-issues-hundreds-orders/story?id=17770090#.UMICaqx hfFw (accessed December 7, 2012).

26. Bennett, "Don't Judge Candidates by Their Faith."

27. TeenagedSasquatch, "Misconceptions of Mormons," *Teen Ink*, n.d., www.teenink.com/ hot_topics/pride_prejudice/article/376630/Misconceptions-of-Mormons/ (accessed March 1, 2012).

HOMOPHOBIA—
A VIRULENT FORM
OF BIGOTRY

"Our voices, our opinions, our primary outlets of communication are the strongest vehicle for change we possess."—Teenage blogger Jenna after speaking out for a LGBT classmate[1]

In June 2011, Iowa teenager Ben Alley graduated from high school. But unlike most graduates, he had no family to help him celebrate. In fact, he has been on his own since he was sixteen years old. That year he told his Southern Baptist parents he was gay, and they kicked him out of their home. He recalled that his mother told him, "You don't even deserve to be alive right now." Nevertheless Alley went on to support himself and was honored with the Matthew Shepard and First Friday Breakfast Club scholarships that are given to gay, lesbian, bisexual, or transgender young leaders. His scholarships helped him enroll at the University of Iowa.[2]

The Matthew Shepard scholarship is named for the twenty-one-year-old man who was tied to a fence in a rural area near Laramie, Wyoming. He was beaten and left to die in 1998 because of his sexual orientation. A month after the crime, members of the Tectonic Theater Project in California traveled to Laramie and conducted interviews with local residents. From these interviews they wrote *The Laramie Project*, which went on to become one of the most performed plays in America. Yet, when students at Notre Dame High School in Lawrence, New Jersey, planned to stage the play in spring 2012, school officials cancelled the production. Reportedly, some parents who complained about the play mistakenly thought it promoted homosexuality, while others thought it was too violent. Some students made polite calls to a talk radio show to say they "felt they had been

Gay men and boys often are subjected to harassment and sometimes brutal physical attacks.

robbed of an opportunity to make the world a better place by shedding light on bigotry and intolerance," reported Bob Ingle in an online feature.[3]

An epilogue *The Laramie Project: 10 Years Later* is a staged reading that was first performed simultaneously in more than one hundred cities worldwide in October 2009. The epilogue focuses on the long-term effects of the murder of Matthew Shepard on the Wyoming town where he lived—and on the nation as a whole. The play includes follow-up interviews with many of the show's original subjects, as well as comments from Matthew's mother, Judy Shepard, and his murderer, Aaron McKinney.

The Laramie Project and a movie with the same title brought attention to hate crimes against homosexuals. But, as an *ABC News* report once noted, "For every Matthew Shepard, there are probably scores of other gay hate crime victims nearly no one has heard about." Many homosexual youth are threatened or injured at school and that has a negative impact on their education not to mention their emotional well-being. In 2010, the National Coalition of Anti-Violence Programs (NCAVP) gathered information on a total of 2,503 survivors and issued a report titled *Violence against Lesbian, Gay, Bisexual, Transgender, Queer, and HIV [LGBTQH]-Affected Communities in the United States in 2010*. It states, "In 2010, anti-LGBTQH violence received unprecedented national attention due to several high profile LGBTQH youth suicides, anti-LGBTQH hate violence attacks and murders, and the increased visibility of anti-LGBTQH bullying."[4] The report concludes,

> Anti-LGBTQH violence persists and is increasingly more severe. Anti-LGBTQH murder is at the second highest level in a decade demonstrating that the homophobic, biphobic, and transphobic culture continues within the U.S. For the first time NCAVP analyzed the individual experiences of LGBTQH survivors and victims of violence to understand the impact of multiple forms of bias on violence. This person-level data highlighted that people of color and transgender people experienced the highest rates of hate violence with the least access to support services, an untenable and life-threatening combination. The 2010 report illustrates what NCAVP member programs have long known, that communities facing long histories of discrimination and violence experienced increased rates of violence.[5]

Some hate crimes reported in recent years include

- the 2008 killing of Larry King, an Oxnard, California, gay teenager, by a classmate, seventeen-year-old Brandon McInerney, who was convicted in November 2011 of second-degree murder and voluntary manslaughter and sentenced to twenty-one years in prison.
- the Latin King Goonies in the Bronx, who, in 2010, abducted a man and tortured him, whipping him with a chain and sodomizing him with a small baseball bat while shouting gay slurs.
- a Massachusetts man beaten in May 2011 by nine people who yelled anti-gay slurs.
- six New York teenagers, in June 2011, allegedly beating and stomping to death an eighteen-year-old thought to be homosexual.
- a teenager in Asheville, North Carolina, and three others allegedly assaulting a man in July 2011; they perceived the victim to be gay.
- a gay couple living in Seattle, Washington, had their tires slashed in September 2011 and a hate message left on their home's front door.

Suicides Because of Gay Bigotry

On September 22, 2010, Tyler Clementi, a freshman at Rutgers University at Piscataway, New Jersey, jumped from the George Washington Bridge, killing himself. According to news stories, Clementi's roommate, Dharun Ravi, and a friend,

"Don't Ask, Don't Tell" Debate

The Don't Ask, Don't Tell (known as DADT) directive was initiated in 1993 and passed in 1994 during the administration of President Bill Clinton. DADT repealed the military policy of prohibiting anyone who had a "propensity or intent to engage in homosexual acts" from serving in the U.S. armed forces. The Clinton administration's new directive ordered the military to refrain from asking any applicant about his or her sexual orientation, because knowing that homosexuals were present "would create an unacceptable risk to the high standards of morale, good order and discipline, and unit cohesion that are the essence of military capability." Nevertheless, people did ask, and thousands of military personnel were investigated, harassed, and discharged.

Many in uniform believed that DADT forced them to live a lie, and the policy was hotly debated across the nation. Those against homosexuals in the military argued in the media, in print materials, on blogs, and on other Internet sites that it was immoral and simply wrong to allow homosexuals to serve. However, by the end of 2010, the U.S. Congress had repealed the law with the backing of a large majority of Americans who approved the action.

In June 2012, the Pentagon held a ceremony to honor LGBT (lesbian, gay, bisexual, and transgender) service members during Gay Pride month. U.S. Defense Secretary Leon Panetta said in a taped message to the gathering, "Before the repeal of Don't Ask Don't Tell you faithfully served your country with professionalism and courage. And just like your fellow service members, you put your country before yourself. . . . And now after repeal you can be proud of serving your country and be proud of who you are when in uniform."[6]

Molly Wei, set up a webcam to spy on and transmit images of a sexual encounter between Clementi and another man. The webcam was placed in Clementi's dorm room, and after he learned about it, he committed suicide. Ravi was charged and convicted of a hate crime in March 2012.

Using digital technology is a way that many students can spy on their peers and post what they find on the Internet. According to a report in the *Christian Science*

Monitor, "Spreading information and images online can make it more emotionally wrenching than . . . more-localized forms of sharing—such as posting embarrassing photos on a bulletin board. . . . Digital images can be cached on the Web, and they can pop up when a person's name is searched." The report further points out that some "observers of youth culture and media culture believe the media environment—including reality shows that use hidden cameras—is desensitizing young people to the hurtful effects of their actions."[7]

Clementi tragically was not the only gay teenager who has committed suicide in recent years. In California, a thirteen-year-old hanged himself because of taunting and harassment he endured for being gay. Nineteen-year-old Raymond Chase, an openly gay student at Johnson & Wales University in Providence, Rhode Island, hanged himself in his dorm room. Fifteen-year-old Billy Lucas of Indiana hung himself after being called an antigay slur over and over in school. Thirteen-year-old Seth Walsh of California killed himself because of taunts about being homosexual.

One sixteen-year-old student, Steven, attempted suicide by taking an overdose of medications, but he survived and was hospitalized. Before that intervention, he wrote a long suicide note for his mom and dad; the note was reprinted verbatim (with misspellings and excessive profanity) on the website Suicide.org. He began,

I am sorry to the people that I love but I cant . . . take it anymore. So I am gay. Why dooes everyone hate me becaus of that. . . . I have been punched and spit on and called faggot, queer, loser. . . . I just am going to end eveythihng now this is it I need to kill myself I love many people mom and dad I love you and you didn't do anything bad I hate life and this is why I have to die I am scared and iam tired of being laughted at made fun of beaten up and threatened.[8]

In Minnesota's Anoka-Hennepin School District, numerous teenagers ended their lives between 2010 and 2012 because of bullying. Some were harassed because they were gay or perceived to be homosexual. Among them: T. J. Hayes, Samantha Johnson, Aaron Jurek, Nick Lockwood, Kevin Buckman, July Barrick, Justin Aaberg, Cole Wilson, and Jordan Yenor. "Suicide rates among gay and lesbian kids are frighteningly high, with attempt rates four times that of their straight counterparts," wrote Sabrina Rubin Erdely in *Rolling Stone*. "Studies show that one-third of all gay youth have attempted suicide at some point (versus 13 percent of hetero kids), and that internalized homophobia contributes to suicide risk." Homophobia is internalized by LGBT people when they begin to believe they are worthless, because of all the negative and insulting words and images hurled at them.

The magazine article continues, "Anoka-Hennepin school district finds itself in the spotlight not only for the sheer number of suicides but because it is accused of having contributed to the death toll by cultivating an extreme anti-gay climate." That climate has been fostered by ultra conservatives and evangelicals who had a set agenda to prevent any discussion of homosexuality in schools and claimed that homosexuals were "sick," sinful, and to blame for their problems and suicides. For years, the school board policy in schools was known as No Homo Promo, which left school officials unable to counteract or help young homosexuals from being verbally and physically attacked. But that policy was questioned after

a student named Alex Merritt filed a complaint with the state Department of Human Rights claiming he'd been gay-bashed by two of his teachers during high school; according to the complaint, the teachers had announced in front of students that Merritt, who is straight, "swings both ways," speculated that he wore women's clothing, and compared him to a Wisconsin man who had sex with a dead deer. The teachers denied the charges, but the school district paid $25,000 to settle the complaint. Soon representatives from the gay-rights group Outfront Minnesota began making inquiries at board meetings. "No Homo Promo" was starting to look like a risky policy.[9]

Eventually the policy changed, but the controversy over whether or not homosexual students should be protected continues.

Gay Marriage Attacks

At Bridgewater State University in Massachusetts, an editorial in the school newspaper favored gay marriage, causing a problem for the writer. In a February 2012 edition of student newspaper the *Comment*, Destinie Mogg-Barkalow, stated, "Prop 8 generates more hate." She referred to the ban on gay marriage in California, calling it intolerant and bigoted. The ban was overturned on February 8 as unconstitutional and a violation of the civil rights of gay and lesbian couples. But Mogg-Barkalow's editorial sparked an attack. According to a report in *EnterpriseNews.com*, a Bridgewater online newspaper, "Mogg-Barkalow told police that she was walking in a campus parking lot . . . when she was approached by a tall man and a shorter woman with red hair who appeared to be fellow students. The two asked Mogg-Barkalow, who was wearing a *Comment* sweatshirt at the time, if she wrote for the newspaper and if she wrote the pro-gay marriage editorial. . . . When she said yes, the woman punched her in the face, leaving a bruise."[10] After university officials and students learned of the attack, they rallied behind Mogg-Barkalow and campus police released a sketch based on Mogg-Barkalow's

> **? Did You Know?**
>
> At one time the American Psychological Association categorized homosexuality as a mental disorder, but after years of research that provided evidence to the contrary, the association in 1973 dropped homosexuality from the disorder category. There is still debate, however, over whether homosexuality is environmental or biological. A person's sex and gender identity are determined long before they reach puberty, before the child surrounds himself or herself with a selected group of comrades. Contrary to common belief, the meaning of sex and gender are not synonymous, nor interchangeable. The X and Y chromosomes of the male and female parents determine the sex of the baby. They may even help to determine the offspring's sexual orientation. Many believe gender to be the result of the environment and nurture children receive, whereas others believe gender is the result of nature and the biological factors or hormones that affected the developing brain. Because there is lengthy research on both sides of the debate, the nature versus nurture argument no doubt will go on indefinitely.

description of the couple, which was published in *EnterpriseNews.com*. The incident could be designated a hate crime, a felony.

Physical attacks based on someone's opposition to gay marriage may not be as prevalent as verbal assaults that frequently become bitter and raucous. This is apparent at rallies for proposed laws to legalize same-sex marriages, some of which are shown in video tapes on YouTube and other Internet sites. Opponents of same-sex marriage, which include religious leaders and politicians, claim that homosexuality is a sin, is immoral and unnatural, and that the Bible condones only marriage between a man and a woman. On the other side, proponents of marriage between two people of the same gender contend their civil rights are being violated when they cannot choose whom to marry and that they are being opposed by bigots who expect everyone to believe as they do.

Many so-called Bible-based Christians (as well as some other religious groups) have launched crusades against legalizing same-sex marriage. Those who cite biblical injunctions against homosexuals marrying appear to dictate who should be legally wed. "Many complained that they weren't anti-gay, that they just opposed same-sex marriage because the Bible, they said, defines marriage as between a man and a woman," wrote Kirsten Powers in *USA Today*. "Yet, we don't live in a theocracy. The Bible is not the governing legal document of the United States. The Constitution is." Powers pointed out that if the Bible were the nation's legal document, divorce would be extremely limited and sex outside of marriage would be banned. In short, she noted the hypocrisy and asked, "Has anyone noticed that there is this special little area carved out where the Bible's teachings must be enshrined in U.S. law, but only when it applies to others, i.e. gay people?"[11]

In 2011, a resolution was brought before the Iowa House of Representatives in an attempt to ban same-sex marriage in the state. (Same-sex marriage has been legal in Iowa since 2009.) But nineteen-year-old Zach Wahls, an engineering student at the University of Iowa, spoke to the legislators, explaining that he was raised by two women. "If I was your son, Mr. Chairman, I believe I would make you very proud," Wahls said. "I'm not really so different from any of your children. My family really isn't so different from yours. . . . The sense of family comes from the commitment we make to each other to work through the hard times so we can enjoy good ones. It comes from the love that binds us. That's what makes a family."[12] The resolution passed the house but not the Iowa senate.

Another teenager, Madison Galluccio of North Haledon, New Jersey, went before the New Jersey state assembly on February 3, 2012, to make an emotional and personal plea to legalize same-sex marriage. Madison and her fathers are made to feel unequal and outcasts in New Jersey, she told the legislators. "But guess what New Jersey. I'm no outcast. I'm Madison Galluccio and I'm part of the Galluccio family," she said. "My parents will be married, and I'll make sure that this happens 'til the day I die." She continued through tears, "So please will you help me? Help me feel equal. We aren't different. I'm not different and I shouldn't have to be forced to feel like I'm different. This is my family and I want us to have the same as the rest of you. So New Jersey please give me my freedom. Thank you."[13]

In mid-February 2012, the New Jersey state senate and assembly passed a bill that recognizes same-sex marriages, but Governor Chris Christie vetoed the legislation. The governor wants the state's citizens to vote on the issue. New Jersey legislators can override the governor's veto, but two-thirds of the lawmakers in the assembly and senate must agree to override. Many political pundits say this is not likely to happen.

Adoption is also an issue for homosexual couples in some states. Same-sex couples cannot adopt in Mississippi, and other states have set up barriers to adoption such as bans against same-sex marriage, which leaves families with limited or no legal protections. Nevertheless, there has been a steady rise in the percentage of same-sex couples who have adopted children, from 10 percent in 2000 to 19 percent in 2009, according to an analysis by the National Council of Family

Where Same-Sex Marriages Are Legal

Most states prohibit same-sex marriage. According to a report by the National Conference of State Legislatures in February 2012, the states

> define marriage in their state constitution and/or state law in a way simi-
> lar to the language in the federal Defense of Marriage Act (DOMA)—"the
> word 'marriage' means only a legal union between one man and one
> woman as husband and wife." Other states prohibit same-sex marriages
> or marriages between persons of the same sex or gender. Twenty-eight
> states have placed that language in their state constitutions (twenty-five
> of these states also have statutory provisions adopting this language).
> A further ten states have statutory language adopting the restrictive
> language. Massachusetts, Connecticut, Iowa, Vermont, New Hampshire,
> New York and the District of Columbia legally allow same-sex marriages.
> Legislation passed in Washington and Maryland in February 2012 will
> allow same-sex marriages, but those laws have not yet taken effect. In
> California, a federal appeals court found that the state constitution's
> restriction on same-sex marriage was invalid, but has postponed enforce-
> ment pending appeal."[14]

Relations. The increase in adoptions by same-sex couples has been related to the fact that tens of thousands of children are waiting to be adopted and the fact that there is more social acceptance of LGBT people.

Cooper, who was a student at Berkeley in 2006, has two mothers, and he says that "a lot of people thought when you come from a gay family, doesn't that make you gay? But I'm not and a bunch of other people I know aren't. . . . I'm extremely lucky to have two parents [who] care about me." That sentiment was shared by two other teenagers, who appeared with Cooper in a DailyMotion.com video. All appeared to be well-adjusted teens who have thrived in their house-holds with same-sex parents.[15]

Same-sex marriage is legal in only a half-dozen states. Where such marriages do occur a wedding cake might hold two bride figurines on top.

What Do You Think?

In early 2012, a Wisconsin Shawano High School student Brandon Wegner was asked to write an opinion piece for the school newspaper. The article was part of opposing viewpoints on the subject of gay adoption. Wegner took the opposition view. Another student's article was in support. Wegner wrote, in part, "Jesus states in the Bible that homosexuality is [a] detestable act and sin which makes adopting wrong for homosexuals because you would be raising a child in a sin filled environment." He added that "same-sex partners adopting children robs children of the potential of growing up with a traditional family consisting of a mom and dad." Wegner cited a number of sources to support his views, including biblical verses and the Family Research Institute. He concluded, "A child needs a mom and dad because that's how God intended it to be."[16]

On the other side, the newspaper editor Maddie Marquardt opined that "American society should not sit back and judge whether or not a person is a suitable parent simply by their sexual orientation." She declared that "homosexuals are human beings, who are as compassionate, caring, and suitable parents as heterosexuals."[17]

Wegner's article prompted "a gay couple whose child attends the school" to lodge a complaint, according to a *Fox News* report, which added,

> The school immediately issued an apology—stating Wegner's opinion was a "form of bullying and disrespect."
>
> "Offensive articles cultivating a negative environment of disrespect are not appropriate or condoned by the Shawano School District," the statement read. "We sincerely apologize to anyone we may have offended and are taking steps to prevent items of this nature from happening in the future."

Beyond this apology, the superintendent of the school district ordered Wegner to his office, where he was questioned about his views. The superintendent reportedly told Wegner he had "to be one of the most ignorant kids to try to argue with him about this topic." Wegner's attorney noted that the superintendent did not stop there—he threatened to suspend Wegner, but that did not happen.[18]

Was the apology and intimidation of a student for expressing his opinion a form of bigotry? What do you think?

Reducing Attacks

Attempts to reduce attacks against homosexuals have taken varied forms. State laws are one attempt. In October 2011, for example, California governor Jerry Brown signed legislation called Seth's Law, named for the young teen who committed suicide because of intimidation for being homosexual. The law requires California school districts to implement policies and procedures for reporting and addressing complaints of harassment against students. At least eighteen other states have passed similar laws.

In some colleges and high schools, students have conducted a Day of Silence to advocate tolerance and acceptance of homosexual students. Day of Silence began in 1996 at the University of Virginia, where more than 150 students participated. The project was designed to create safe schools for all, regardless of sexual orientation, and to support the rights of LGBT people. Students vowed to remain silent all day and carried cards explaining why they would not speak. By remaining silent, the students demonstrated that many LGBT people have no voice and must keep their sexual preferences secret—that is, remain in the closet—to avoid harassment, prejudice, discrimination, and even violence.

Student Maria Pulzetti, who was eighteen years old at the time, was motivated to nationalize the Day of Silence. Pulzetti and nineteen-year-old Jessie Gilliam developed the project to be used in schools across the country. They initiated a website and the idea spread across the United States and to other countries. In April each year, hundreds of thousands of students participate in the national Day of Silence. The cards they carry say,

Please understand my reasons for not speaking today. I am participating in the Day of Silence, a national youth movement bringing attention to the silence faced by lesbian, gay, bisexual and transgender people and their allies in schools. My deliberate silence echoes that silence, which is caused by name-calling, bullying and harassment. I believe that ending the silence is the first step toward fighting these injustices. Think about the voices you are not hearing today. What are you going to do to end the silence?[19]

In 2008, the national Day of Silence was dedicated to a gay teenager, Lawrence King of Oxnard, California, who was shot and killed by a schoolmate Brandon McInerney. The director of the Transgender Law Center in Ventura County where Oxnard is located told a reporter that Brandon was "just as much a victim as Lawrence. He's a victim of homophobia and hate."[20]

In April 2011, one of the Day of Silence participants was Meghann G., who was jeered by some of her peers. She decided to go to a counselor's office to write about her feelings, which she posted on her blog. In part, she noted,

> The meaning of Day of Silence is so much more powerful when experiencing it, hearing about it doesn't compare. The feeling of isolation puts you in a daze, where you forget about the "importance" of every day conversations. The lack of talking even dries out your throat and when you do speak again your voice cracks on the choked out words.
>
> Day of Silence isn't just a protest against bullying or something to bring attention to others, but it's to bring a more intense, tangible, awareness to the participants. I tell people it's not as hard as it sounds, just to get them to do it, but in all reality it is hard and stressful and saddening to an extent; however it is also enlightening and eye-opening and incredibly, absolutely powerful. Anyone who has participated the whole day would know. It's inspirational.[21]

Apparently the Delaware Valley Regional High School in New Jersey did not agree that the Day of Silence is inspirational. The school cancelled the 2012 event, but one transgender student, Shawn Watkins-Murphy, commented on NJ.com that regardless he would participate. That was greeted with this message from a parent: "These are MY kids educated with MY tax dollars. I choose to raise them MY way. For a public institution to force any kind of worldly views on them is against MY choice. For you to disagree and think that they should is the epitome of intolerance. They are at school to learn reading, writing, etc. Save the liberal 'everybody is equal' BS."

A countering statement noted, "Whether you agree with it or not, the publicity of the issue is allowing the younger generation to become more accepting of the different types of people that make up our country. You can be a bigot, you can loudly disagree with how others live their lives, but the very fact that this issue is in the public eye is just the start of the wave that will eventually crash all over those types of views."[22]

Truth and Refuge?

Programs that counter the Day of Silence once included the Day of Truth, an antigay ministry project that was sponsored by Exodus International, an organization with affiliates such as Love in Action (LIA). LIA once operated a boot camp called Refuge to convince homosexual youth that they have a psychological disorder. Sixteen-year-old Zach Stark of Tennessee was sent to Refuge and his story made international news. It also became the basis for a documentary (released in 2011). He first described what happened on his blog in 2005 when he told his parents he was gay.

> My mother, father, and I had a very long "talk" in my room where they let me know I am to apply for a fundamentalist christian program for gays. They tell me that there is something psychologically wrong with me, and they "raised me wrong." I'm a big screw up to them, who isn't on the path God wants me to be on. So I'm sitting here in tears, joining the rest of those kids who complain about their parents on blogs—and I can't help it.[23]

The blog was circulated widely in the electronic media and created a backlash. Exodus shut down its Refuge program in 2010. The ministry also discontinued its Day of Truth program, an annual event to counter the Day of Silence with messages that homosexual youth are sinful or perverse.

For eight weeks, Zach was in the boot camp where he had to attend counseling and therapy sessions designed to turn him straight. The documentary titled *This Is What Love in Action Looks Like* took six years to develop and shows how Zach's schoolmates supported him by protesting every day outside the camp. Others in the documentary also were forced by their parents to go to the camp and they, too, tell their stories.

Another effort to reduce LGBT harassment is the LGBT-Friendly Campus Climate Index at www.campusclimateindex.org. "The nationally praised Index takes an in-depth look at LGBT-friendly policies, programs and practices," the website declares. In August 2008, more than 230 colleges were "ranked from one to five stars, depending on their answers to a detailed, voluntary questionnaire submitted to Campus Pride, a national non-profit working to create safer, more LGBT-inclusive colleges and build future LGBT and ally leaders. In development since 2001, the Index has become a staple in student and faculty research, campus organizing efforts and benchmarking for LGBT student safety and inclusion on campus."

Off the Bookshelf

Rainbow Boys by Alex Sanchez is a fictional account of three gay high school students: Jason Carrillo, a good-looking jock who questions his sexuality; Kyle Meeks, who is on the swim team, knows he is homosexual, but fears being open about it; and Nelson Glassman, a defiant homosexual who's "out" and appears to revel in his role as "Nelly," wearing numerous earrings, "weird" hairstyles, and "snapping his fingers."[24] Yet Nelson is often a target of bigots who harass him at school.

The three are in their last semester of their senior year. Each chapter follows one of the boys, beginning with Jason, then Kyle, and then Nelson. All three are struggling with issues. Jason has a girlfriend and does not understand why he is attracted to guys. Kyle, who is Nelson's best friend, is infatuated with Jason. And Nelson is in love with Kyle. As their stories progress, each must deal with not only their emotions but also with family and friends. Jason's father is an alcoholic and constantly berates Jason, calling him a weakling. Kyle's parents have difficulty accepting that their son is gay, but they eventually support him. Nelson's mother, a member of Parents, Families, and Friends of Lesbians and Gays (PFLAG) and is supportive, but his father is not around and only shows up on rare occasions to spend any time with Nelson. There also is an HIV scare that affects each of them in one way or another. The story ends with the students attending a Gay-Straight Alliance meeting in the school counselor's conference room.

Campus Pride has listed nineteen campuses with a five-star ranking. These include "Carleton College; Humboldt State University; Ithaca College; Oberlin College; Oregon State University; Princeton University; San Diego State University; Syracuse University; The Ohio State University; The Pennsylvania State University; University of California, Berkeley; University of California, Los Angeles; University of California, Riverside; University of Maine, Farmington; University of Oregon; University of Pennsylvania; University of Southern California; University of Vermont; and Washington University in St. Louis."[25]

Providing novels and nonfiction books for teenagers in schools is another way to counteract homophobia. Frequently, books about LGBTQ teens do not appear in school libraries, but when they do, the books "can be an excellent way to gain a window into the lives of LGBTQ teens—which in and of itself include a massive diversity of experiences based on race, ethnicity, culture, and identity—and increase one's understanding of this important subset of teens," according to the Young Adult Library Services Association. "For readers who do identify as LGBTQ, these titles can be crucial reflections of one's reality and also present different perspectives that can shed light on one's own personal experience."[26]

Notes

1. Jenna, "Speaking through Silence to Stop Hate," *Life and the Teenage Mind* (blog), April 14, 2011, jennasteenmind.blogspot.com/ (accessed June 8, 2012).
2. Jeff, "Iowa Gay Teen Triumphs after Family Disowns Him at 16 Years Old," Proud Parenting, June 11, 2011, www.proudparenting.com/node/16263 (accessed March 8, 2012).
3. Bob Ingle, "Play Would Have Let Kids Hear Powerful Message," *CourierPostOnline.com*, March 29, 2012, partially available at www.mycentraljersey.com/article/20120329/NJCOL-UMNIST06/303290012/Let-kids-hear-powerful-messages-their-way (accessed December 10, 2012).
4. National Coalition of Anti-Violence Programs (NCAVP), *2010 Hate Violence against Lesbian, Gay, Bisexual, Transgender, Queer and HIV-Affected Communities in the United States* (New York: New York City Gay & Lesbian Anti-Violence Project, Inc. 2011), 4.
5. NCAVP, *2010 Hate Violence*, 48.
6. Dana Hughes, "Gay Military Members Honored in First-Ever Pentagon Ceremony," *ABC News*, June 26, 2012, abcnews.go.com/blogs/politics/2012/06/gay-military-members-honored -in-first-ever-pentagon-ceremony/ (accessed June 30, 2012).
7. Stacy Teicher Khadaroo, "Rutgers Student Death: Has Digital Age Made Students Callous?" *Christian Science Monitor*, October 1, 2010, www.csmonitor.com/USA/Society/2010/1001/ Rutgers-student-death-Has-Digital-Age-made-students-callous (accessed March 10, 2012).
8. Kevin Caruso, "Suicide Note of a Gay Teen," Suicide.org, n.d., www.suicide.org/suicide -note-of-a-gay-teen.html (accessed March 10, 2012).

9. Sabrina Rubin Erdely, "One Town's War on Gay Teens," *Rolling Stone*, February 2, 2012, www.rollingstone.com/politics/news/one-towns-war-on-gay-teens-20120202?print=true (accessed March 12, 2012).

10. Justin Graeber, "BSU Student Says She Was Punched over Pro-Gay Marriage Piece," *EnterpriseNews.com*, last updated February 20, 2012, www.enterprisenews.com/answerbook/bridgewater/x306963172/A-Bridgewater-State-student-says-she-was-attacked-over-pro-gay-marriage-article?zc_p=0 (accessed March 13, 2012).

11. Kirsten Powers, "Hypocrisy Shrouds Gay Marriage Debate," *USA Today*, November 8, 2010, www.usatoday.com/news/opinion/forum/2010-11-08-column08_ST_N.htm (accessed March 14, 2012).

12. Lesley Kennedy, "Teen's Impassioned Speech Supporting Gay Marriage in Iowa Goes Viral," ParentDish, February 3, 2011, www.parentdish.com/2011/02/03/gay-marriage-iowa/ (accessed March 17, 2012).

13. Video courtesy NJ.com posted on *Advocate.com*, February 3, 2012, www.advocate.com/News/Daily_News/2012/02/03/WATCH_NJ_Teen_Plead_for_Her_Gay_Dads_Right_to_Marry/ (accessed March 19, 2012).

14. National Conference of State Legislatures, "Defining Marriage: Defense of Marriage Acts and Same-Sex Marriage Laws," updated February 24, 2012, www.ncsl.org/issues-research/human-services/same-sex-marriage-overview.aspx (accessed March 13, 2012).

15. gaysrkool, *I Have Gay Parents* (video), DailyMotion, n.d., www.dailymotion.com/video/xlrr9_i-have-gay-parents_news (accessed March 18, 2012).

16. Brandon Wegner, "Should Homosexual Partners Be Able to Adopt," *GreenBayPressGazette.com*, n.d., www.greenbaypressgazette.com/assets/pdf/U0183892114.PDF (accessed March 4, 2012).

17. Maddie Marquardt, "Who Sets Standards of a Suitable Parent?" *GreenBayPressGazette.com*, n.d., www.greenbaypressgazette.com/assets/pdf/U0183892114.PDF (accessed March 4, 2012).

18. Tod Starnes, "Atty Says School Threatened, Punished Boy Who Opposed Gay Adoption," *Fox News Radio*, January 24, 2012, radio.foxnews.com/toddstarnes/top-stories/atty-says-school-threatened-punished-boy-who-opposed-gay-adoption.html (accessed March 4, 2012).

19. Gay, Lesbian and Straight Education Network, "The History of the Day of Silence®," Day of Silence, n.d., www.dayofsilence.org/content/history.html (accessed March 13, 2012).

20. Rebecca Cathcart, "Boy's Killing, Labeled a Hate Crime, Stuns a Town," *New York Times*, February 23, 2008, www.nytimes.com/2008/02/23/us/23oxnard.html (accessed March 13, 2012).

21. Meghann G., "Day of Silence Student Voices: Meghann G.," *Day of Silence Blog*, April 28, 2011, blog.dayofsilence.org/2011/04/day-of-silence-student-voices-meghann-g.html (accessed March 13, 2012).

22. "Your Comments: Delaware Valley High School's [sic] Cancels 'Day of Silence'; Transgender Student Takes Issue," *Hunterdon County Democrat*, April 21, 2012, blog.nj.com/hunterdon news_impact/print.html?entry=/2012/04/your_comments_delaware_valley.html (accessed August 30, 2012).

23. Mike Airhart, "Antigay Father Outs 'Zach,'" *Ex-Gay Watch*, July 13, 2005, www.exgay watch.com/wp/2005/07/antigay-father/ (accessed December 7, 2012). Also see "Forced Ex-Gay Therapy," gaycopt.blogspot.com/2012/08/forced-ex-gay-therapy.html.

24. Alex Sanchez, *Rainbow Boys* (New York: Simon Pulse/Simon & Schuster, 2003), 2.

25. cpsiteadmin, "Campus Pride Climate Index Ranks Gay-Friendliness of American Colleges and Universities," Campus Pride, August 2, 2010, www.campusprideblog.org/blog/just -announced-campus-pride-climate-index-ranks-gay-friendliness-american-colleges-and -universi (accessed March 13, 2012).

26. Cristina Mitra, "Introducing 'A Different Light': A Spotlight on LGBTQ-themed YA Lit," YALSA: The Hub, September 30, 2011, www.yalsa.ala.org/thehub/2011/09/30/introducing -a-different-light-a-spotlight-on-lgbtq-themed-ya-lit/ (accessed March 15, 2012).

BULLYING

"If I see a certain group of people in the hall, I'll duck my head and walk as far around them as possible so that they don't see me and make fun of me."
—*Jen, a high school junior at Bear River High School, telling a reporter about being bullied[1]*

Tyler Clementi, Raymond Chase, Billy Lucas, Seth Walsh, T. J. Hayes, Samantha Johnson, Aaron Jurek, Nick Lockwood, Kevin Buckman, July Barrick, Justin Aaberg, Cole Wilson, and Jordan Yenor. They were harassed and bullied during the years between 2009 and 2011 because of their homosexuality or perceived homosexuality. They got to the point where they couldn't take it any longer and they wanted to die. They did—by committing suicide. But these young people are not alone in the type of bullying that leads some teenagers to end it all. Phoebe is an example.

Phoebe Prince was fifteen years old in 2010 and a new student at South Hadley High School in Massachusetts. She was from Ireland and like most teenagers she just wanted to fit in and enjoy her high school years. But instead, *ABC News* reported, she endured "nearly three months of routine torment by [six] students at South Hadley High School, via text message, and through the social networking site, Facebook." Reportedly she was "harassed by older girls who resented her dating an older football player." She was called an Irish slut and other derogatory terms. For Phoebe, school life became intolerable and she hung herself in the stairway leading to the apartment on the second floor where the family lived. The girls who harassed Phoebe were indicted for their part in Phoebe's suicide. In addition, two older male students who attacked Phoebe were charged with statutory rape.[2]

Teenager Asher Brown of Texas was bullied often. Some of his classmates taunted him because of his pigeon-toed walk, his lisp, the perception that he was gay, and for being a Buddhist. He also had Asperger's syndrome. Although Asher's parents repeatedly complained to school officials, nothing was done. Shortly after one bully pushed Asher down two flights of stairs at the school, Asher committed suicide in September 2010. His mother filed a lawsuit against the president of the school board in February 2012.[3]

Amanda Cummings was fifteen when she committed suicide. In 2012, she revealed to friends that some students from her New Dorp High School in Staten Island, New York, were bullying her on Facebook and in person. The bullying was in part due to Amanda's lack of conformity—she didn't go along with the crowd. Also she apparently was harassed by a girl who resented Amanda because they both liked the same boy. Amanda wrote a suicide note and jumped in front of a Metropolitan Transportation Authority bus. She was rushed to a hospital but died six days later.

In Palm Bay, Florida, three black teenagers tormented an autistic fifteen-year-old at a school bus stop in February 2012. The white fifteen-year-old, who had often been a victim of bullying, ran out into the street and was almost hit by a truck and motorcycle. The three attackers were charged with a hate crime.

Who Are the Targets?

Students who are targeted for bullying may be verbally or physically attacked because they don't conform in one way or another. Perhaps it is the clothing they wear, speech difficulties, physical disabilities, being overweight or obese, religious apparel, being a serious student ("a nerd"), or even having red hair. For example, teens with red hair may be subjected to what is called ginger abuse. According to an *ABC News* report in 2011, "Ginger abuse has become comedic fodder for the popular cartoon, 'South Park.' The show regularly features its characters harassing redheads, and several years ago started to run an episode which featured a 'Kick a Ginger Day.' Now each year, on November 20, dozens of redheads have reported being kicked by classmates and strangers who have a problem with their hair color."[4]

On a Minnesota social network called Students Speak Out (SOS), a program of the Citizens League (citzensleague.org), students can express their opinions on a variety of issues. Teenagers who participate not only can be heard, but also can help find solutions to civic problems and influence change. In 2008, SOS participants addressed bullying. One university student said she "was bullied all throughout high school. All four years. I would say it was sometimes physical, most of the time mental and emotional. . . . I was considered a nerd because I took a leadership position."[5]

A high school student who took part in SOS noted that "I was in class and people always text and stuff . . . which is normal. But in one of my classes, girls were taking pictures with their phones of this one girl in class who's considered 'nerdy' and 'annoying.' They then proceeded to send the picture around class via text, giggling. She was completely oblivious . . . which almost makes it more disgusting."[6]

Teenager Zach Veach, a seventeen-year-old professional race car driver with Andretti Autosport, was bullied in high school. He told the *Huffington Post* that he had been interested in racing since he was ten years old. As a teenager, he began driving in go-kart competitions in Indianapolis, Indiana, and when he won a race he received a hat. "Being proud like I was, I wore it to school because that was my [first] win in my career. The bullies at lunch were just so mean. One grabbed my hat, threw it in the trashcan, and poured white milk all over it. At the time I was a little upset, but as I look back it's kind of ironic because after you win the Indianapolis 500 they give you milk!" Now he advises kids, "Don't let bullies push you around just because you're different."[7]

Youth and adults who wear religious head coverings may be bullied. Consider Gurwinder Singh, a Sikh from India, who faced bullying all through his school years in Queens, New York. Singh's experiences in high school included a girl dumping soda all over his turban in front of his entire biology class with inadequate response from the teacher. As a Sikh, Singh's turban is a head covering that he must wear as a religious obligation for males of the Punjab region of India. He also was bullied by a group of classmates led by a one-time friend. The group chased him, caught up with him, banged him against a pole in the subway station, and left him bleeding, with no bystander attempting to help him. Singh explained to a *SikhNN* reporter, "I wanted to be able to reach out to people and ask for help. . . . But my parents did not speak English, they could not go to school to explain. There were no interpreters to help them explain." Singh also tried to avoid trouble by keeping to himself. "I always felt lonely and did not want to talk to anybody," he said.[8]

Singh told his story about bullying while at a White House Conference on Bullying Prevention held in March 2011. In opening remarks at the conference, President Obama noted,

> If there's one goal of this conference, it's to dispel the myth that bullying is just a harmless rite of passage or an inevitable part of growing up. It's not. Bullying can have destructive consequences for our young people. And it's not something we have to accept. As parents and students, teachers and communities, we can take steps that will help prevent bullying and create a climate in our schools in which all of our children can feel safe.

President Obama also explained that he was at times a victim of bullying. In his words, "I have to say, with big ears and the name that I have, I wasn't immune. I didn't emerge unscathed."[9]

Overweight or obese teens frequently suffer bullying. Harassment is often a daily occurrence for most young people who are overweight. Even at home they may have brothers, sisters, or other relatives who label them with humiliating terms: *fat chick, ocra, pig, army tank, big chops, fatty-fatty-two-by-four*, and on and on.

On the website I Was a Fat Kid . . . This Is My Story (www.catay.com/fatkid/school.asp), there are numerous accounts of how fat students have been bullied. The stories have a recurring theme—nearly all of the writers hated school because of the belittling abuse they experienced. Most were not defended by teachers or school officials. From Fat-Freedom Fighter comes this story:

> I am 16. I am 240 lbs. I have a 38 inch waist. I have a disease: being fat. I have been fat for most of my life. . . . I am constantly having names and any other things thrown at me. I am always picked last to play sports in gym and I don't even play sports anywhere else anymore, not even at home. I used to play baseball and football but I couldn't take the harassment from peers and coaches anymore. I am especially sick of this one asshole named Brandon. He was my friend until he got skinny. Now the only thing that escapes his mouth towards me is, "Hey, look at Adam's tits. they are bigger than Britney Spears'."[10]

In the workforce, overweight teens and adults may also face harassment and discrimination. According to a study sponsored by the Rudd Center for Food Policy and Obesity at Yale University, weight bias "remains very socially acceptable in our culture." Published in 2008, the study concluded that weight discrimination—frequently referred to as weightism—is on the rise in the United States. The study is based on participants' reports of discrimination they had experienced. These self-reports "revealed that women are twice as likely as men to experience weight discrimination and that weight discrimination in the workplace and interpersonal mistreatment due to obesity is common."[11]

A study by Michigan State University researchers came to similar conclusions. In that study, 2,838 workers reported bias in the workplace, with weight discrimination the most common form, topping "discrimination based on sex, age, race, ethnicity, sexual orientation, religion or disability."[12]

Cyberbullying

Social networking websites, blogs, online videos, text messages, iPhone photos, and video games are all part of the media that have been used for bullying in cyberspace—cyberbullying. "In the old days, when a teenager said something

Two Books Off the Shelf: The Fat Boy Chronicles *and* Odd Girl Speaks Out

The Fat Boy Chronicles by Michael Buchanan and Diane Lang is a novel inspired by a true story. In a first-person journal format, teenager Jimmy Winterpock, who happens to be fat, tells how he endures bullying from his classmates. One entry begins,

> Today I was in the gym when it started again with the guys in the locker room. Of course, there's never anyone around, but I don't want teachers to have to protect me. I'd like to fight back but I know I'd get pounded on, big time. "Melon Boy" and "Man-Boobs," they yell at me. I hate it and it makes my neck turn red. The worst is Robb. Apparently he comes to school for the purpose of playing football and making my life miserable. Today, he said, "Hey, Jimmy, are you gellin', because I see your melons!"[13]

As the story proceeds through the journal, which is an English assignment to write three half-pages each week, Jimmy tells about one incident after another in which some of his classmates—both male and female teenagers—tease, taunt, call him names, and make his life miserable. However, he does have a friend at school, Allen, who is as heavy as Jimmy and is also bullied.

Another friend, Paul, lives close by but goes to another school. When a dead body is found near Paul's house, Paul decides to play detective and gets Jimmy involved—though reluctantly—in a hunt for the murderer. This mystery weaves through the story and eventually causes the boys some problems. In addition, Paul has his own problems with his dysfunctional family.

On the upbeat side of the story, Jimmy begins to find ways to lose weight. He stops eating junk food, diets, runs, and works out with his father. It's a long struggle, but before the end of the school year he has succeeded in dropping sixty pounds. Jimmy also finds a girlfriend and develops an unexpected friendship with Robb, his former bully. Jimmy and Robb are in the same math class and Robb needs help with algebra in order to pass finals and earn a football scholarship. The math teacher asks Jimmy to tutor Robb. "At first, Robb was a real jerk—almost as bad as he was earlier in the year—but when he saw I really could help him, he eased up and started joking around about how clueless he was in math," Jimmy says in his journal.[14] The two end up not only studying algebra but also working out together. It's a win-win situation for both of them.

Odd Girl Speaks Out: Girls Write about Bullies, Cliques, Popularity, and Jealousy is a collection of true accounts edited by Rachel Simmons and published in paperback. All the stories are anonymous; only the ages of the writers appear. For example, a twenty-one-year-old woman describes how she was bullied in middle school because of her weight, and then in high school she became a bully herself. As she wrote, "I thought if I pretended to be strong, and if I picked on everyone else that was weaker than me, no one would see the chubby girl that was tortured just years earlier. I felt as long as I was making fun of someone else, they couldn't turn the tables and make fun of me." The storyteller later ran into Monica, one of the girls she had bullied, and learned that Monica had developed an eating disorder because of the bullying. As a result, the writer "was left with the horrible realization that I had become the very type of person I hated. I was my own worst nightmare."[15]

Other accounts also describe bullying incidents. A sixteen-year-old noted that she "was a bully in the sense that I would hang out with my louder friends when we all confronted someone we didn't like. I was a bully by association. I never really did the verbal confrontation myself. I just stood by and let it happen."[16]

The book contains letters, poems, and essays from girls across the United States. Throughout the book, Rachel Simmons advises readers on the problems they have faced. Simmons explains in an introductory note that "the stories are published [in the book] in order to provide a public space for girls to discuss a part of their lives that is often silenced. . . . Every girl writes from her own vantage point. . . . Please keep in mind that the authors' opinions are not intended as the last word on any incident, only as a snapshot of their lives."[17]

---

regrettable, it was unfortunate and emotionally painful—with the embarrassment usually lasting for a day or two. Now, though, off the cuff remarks sent in text form can immediately go viral, and brief social exchanges can make their way on to U-tube [*sic*]—where they remain forever indelible. There are no take-backs in cyber space," wrote Stephanie Newman in *Psychology Today*.[18] The National Crime Prevention Council says that "an overwhelming majority of teens believe

Both males and females may take part in some form of bullying.

True or False?

- Bullies are likely to pick on those who are physically smaller than they are and have little social power.
- A bully could be someone who has at one time or another been bullied.
- A bully may spread malicious rumors about someone or call another person derogatory names.
- Both males and females may take part in some form of bullying.
- Some bullies are popular and may be proud of their aggressive behavior and their power to control other people.
- If students and teachers ignore bullying, the bullies believe they can continue to act with impunity.
- School initiatives to prevent and stop bullying have reduced bullying by 15 to 50 percent. The most successful initiatives to stop bullying in schools involve the entire staff, parents, students, and community members.[19]

All of the above statements are true.

Teenagers and young adults who have Internet access and cell phones could be bullying victims or could be bullies themselves.

that youth cyberbully because they think it's a joke, not realizing the negative impact it may have on the victim. Many teens also think that youth cyberbully because they are encouraged by friends or because they believe that everyone else cyberbullies."[20] Maggie Flick, a high school junior in Jackson, Michigan, writes a weekly blog for *Mlive* and in February 2012 had this to say about teenagers and cyberbullying:

> Sometimes, we get a little trapped inside of our world and don't notice when we hurt others. We'll post something on Facebook or Twitter without even realizing it might offend someone. The people who do it on accident are the ones who regret it. They feel bad and apologize for what they did. . . . Some people intentionally cyber bully, and they don't just post a single status. They post one every day. They write mean wall posts, send cruel messages, and comment on pictures saying the meanest of mean things.

In her blog Flick points out that not all people who cyberbully are mean in real life. "They'll hurt others because they are secretly hurting themselves." Her final advice: "Think before you speak or post. Words hurt, make sure yours don't."[21]

On the social news site *reddit*, Sarah asked for help dealing with a bully, a popular male student who was harassing her, stating that she had to threaten suicide to get the attention of school authorities at Arundel High School in Gambrills, Maryland. Sarah, who did not give her last name, wrote that the bully repeatedly sent her messages online and in person, such as, "Go kill yourself. No one would care if you died. Why aren't you dead yet?" or "Please do us a favor, and f-g drown," or "Sarah for biggest slut. Go die." In her *reddit* message, she wrote,

As a teenager dealing with depression and suicidal thoughts, I could not laugh this off. I went straight to the office and demanded to see a vice principal. I was sobbing uncontrollably and visibly a danger to myself, but they just sat me down and had me fill out a form. I called my Dad, who cancelled his flight out-of-town to come be with me. He was furious that he was not called in a situation like this. We had a conference with the vice principal, and we were told there would be consequences if it happened again.[22]

So many people responded with e-mails and phone calls to the school that in a short time, Sarah was able to write with emphasis in capital letters that the bully "has been suspended until the school decides what to do with him. Thank you for your support and emails, but THERE IS NO NEED FOR ANYONE TO EMAIL THE SCHOOL ANY FURTHER!!!! The matter is being taken seriously now, and everything can move a lot quicker if the school isn't being flooded with email and concern. I promise you, action has been taken. Thank you!"[23]

In Connecticut, cyberbullying occurred in January 2012 in the form of homophobic slurs against a Ridgefield High School student. But fellow classmates took action to stop the bullying. Led by senior Sophie Needleman, students created a Facebook page called "Southern Connecticut High Schools: An End to Cyber Bullying." More than nine hundred members joined the cause within twenty-four hours.[24] Later a new page was formed called "Students against Internet Discrimination: An End to Cyber Bullying." By the end of June 2012, the page had received 1,264 likes.

Forty-eight states have passed varied laws to protect people against bullying, but many "states have enacted 'cyberstalking' or 'cyberharassment' laws or have laws that explicitly include electronic forms of communication within more traditional stalking or harassment laws. In addition, recent concerns about protecting minors from online bullying or harassment have led states to enact 'cyberbullying' laws," reports the National Conference of State Legislatures.[25] For example, one part of the California law states that "bullying, including bullying committed personally or by means of an electronic act . . . includes the posting of messages on a social network Internet Website." Seth's Law, which became effective in July 2012, "strengthens existing policies in California schools by requiring that all schools have an anti-bullying policy and . . . enacts a timeline that school officials must follow when investigating student claims of bullying," according to the *Sacramento Press*.[26]

Sexual Harassment in Schools

Passed in 1972, Title IX of the 1964 Civil Rights Act explicitly prohibited sexual harassment in schools. An amendment to Title IX was passed in 1992 and received widespread public attention, in part because of a U.S. Supreme Court decision that same year. The case, *Franklin v. Gwinnett County Public Schools*, involved a Georgia teenager who charged that a teacher had consistently harassed her during a time when she helped him grade papers. According to the suit, the teacher wanted to know about the teenager's sex life, discussed his own, and eventually persuaded her to have sex with him. The justices ruled in favor of the teenager and unanimously declared that students can be awarded monetary damages for sex discrimination and sexual harassment.

Unfortunately, the 1992 case is not unique. Over the years, teachers, coaches, and other authority figures in schools have taken advantage of students' vulnerability and emerging awareness of their sexuality and have abused their relationships with young girls and boys. That is the accusation against the former Penn State football coach Jerry Sandusky. In November 2011 Sandusky was charged with molesting ten young boys whom he befriended through a charity called Second Mile, giving them presents and taking them to sporting events. A reporter for Reuters notes, "Sandusky is alleged to have had physical contact with the boys ranging from tickling and a 'soap battle' in Penn State showers to oral and anal sex." In 2012, a jury convicted him on forty-five of forty-eight counts related to sexual abuse of boys.

All public and private education institutions that receive any federal funds must comply with Title IX. Under Title IX, students are protected from harassment connected to any of the academic, extracurricular, athletic, or other programs or activities of schools, regardless of the location. The U.S. Department of Education Office of Civil Rights defines sexual harassment as conduct that

1. is sexual in nature;
2. is unwelcome; and
3. denies or limits a student's ability to participate in or benefit from a school's education program.

Sexual harassment can take different forms depending on the harasser and the nature of the harassment. The conduct can be carried out by school employees, other students, and non-employee third parties, such as a visiting speaker. Both male and female students can be victims of sexual harassment and the harasser and the victim can be of the same sex.

The conduct can occur in any school program or activity and can take place in school facilities, on a school bus, or at other off-campus locations, such as a school-sponsored field trip or a training program at another location.[27]

While sexual harassment is a form of bullying (sexual bullying) the terms have different definitions and "are regulated by different laws. Too often, the more comfortable term *bullying* is used to describe sexual harassment, obscuring the role of gender and sex in these incidents," according to the American Association of University Women (AAUW). Certainly the teenagers who committed suicide because of their sexual orientation were sexually harassed as well as bullied. And someone like Sarah who was called a slut by a bully was both sexually harassed and bullied. TeenHealth.org, a website that is reviewed by doctors, makes the distinction between sexual harassment and sexual bullying:

Sexual harassment and sexual bullying . . . both involve unwelcome or unwanted sexual comments, attention, or physical contact. So why call one thing by two different names?

Sometimes schools and other places use one term or the other for legal reasons. For instance, a school document may use the term "bullying" to describe what's against school policy, while a law might use the term "harassment" to define what's against the law. Some behaviors might be against school policy and also against the law.[28]

According to AAUW's survey of 1,965 seventh through twelfth grade students,

Sexual harassment is part of everyday life in middle and high schools. Nearly half (48 percent) of the students surveyed experienced some form of sexual harassment in the 2010–11 school year, and the majority of those students (87 percent) said it had a negative effect on them. Verbal harassment (unwelcome sexual comments, jokes, or gestures) made up the bulk of the incidents, but physical harassment was far too common. Sexual harassment by text, e-mail, Facebook, or other electronic means affected nearly one-third (30 percent) of students. Interestingly, many of

It's a Fact

For years it has been commonly believed that women and girls "provoke" or invite sexual remarks and harassment, and that girls should behave and dress properly to assure that they will be treated with respect. In other words, the assumption is that females are responsible if they are sexually harassed. Even now, such myths prevail. But the fact is that sexual harassment occurs no matter how girls and women dress. That has been true for women in uniform, in conservative business suits and attire, and in medical garb.

the students who were sexually harassed through cyberspace were also sexually harassed in person.[29]

Workplace Bullying

While bullying in schools is well publicized and laws prohibit it, the same cannot be said about bullying in the workplace. However, Healthy Workplace bills have been proposed in numerous states to address the issue. About the only recourse a worker has against a bully is a company policy that forbids or at least discourages bullying behavior.

"Workplace bullying is when a person or group of people in a workplace single out another person for unreasonable, embarrassing, or intimidating treatment," states the Bullying Statistics website. The bully is likely a person in an authority position, someone who feels threatened by the victim. "In some cases, the bully is a co-worker who is insecure or immature. Workplace bullying can be the result of a single individual acting as a bully or of a company culture that allows or even encourages this kind of negative behavior."[30]

Young people just entering the workforce seldom are targets for bullying—they don't have the power on the job to affect the status of older workers, although they do have recourse if they are targets of sexual harassment or racial bullying, which are illegal.

In 2007, the Workplace Bullying Institute (WBI) commissioned Zogby International to conduct a survey of 7,740 adult Americans on the topic of workplace bullying. Three years later in 2010, Zogby conducted two surveys: "one with several items and 4,210 survey respondents and one single-item survey with 2,092 respondents." WBI then compared the results and found that "bullying remains a problem for over a third of the population." In addition the data showed, "Both

It Happened to Katy Butler

Seventeen-year-old Katy Butler of Michigan became an activist against bullying after being victimized while attending middle school in Plymouth, near Ann Arbor. She became a target when students learned that she is a lesbian. She recalled for the *Daily Beast*, "Kids ended up walking down the hallway, calling me names, pushing me against walls and into lockers, knocking my books over. Horrible things like that. Their favorite name to call me was definitely 'fag'—that was used a lot. Also: 'dyke.' They ended up slamming my hand into my locker one day and breaking my finger."

Katy's parents sent her to a private high school in Ann Arbor and in 2011 she joined with some state legislators who were trying to get an antibullying law passed. Then she heard that a documentary film on bullying had been produced and thought that could be a positive force. The documentary, *Bully*, follows five students who are bullied during the school year 2009–2010. But the film was rated R, which is set by the Motion Picture Association, because harsh profanity is used by bullies against victims. The R rating meant that anyone under age seventeen could not see the film without a parent or guardian. "I thought that was really counterproductive because it prevents most of the kids that need to see it from actually seeing it," Katy noted. "So I went on Change.org and started a petition to change the movie's rating to PG-13."[31]

As of the end of March 2012, nearly five hundred thousand people had signed the petition, but that did not change the rating. And the award-wining film director Lee Hirsh refused to cut the profanity in the film so it could receive a PG-13 rating. As a result, Weinstein Company, the film's distributor, decided to release *Bully* without a rating; it opened in New York and Los Angeles on March 31, 2012, and went on to be shown in twenty-five other cities. Although there have been warnings that some movie theaters won't show the film because it lacks a rating, Katy Butler was not upset. She noted that every day kids who are bullied hear the ugly language and suffer the attacks as shown in the film.

men and women bully, but the majority of bullying is same-gender harassment, which is mostly legal according to anti-discrimination laws and workplace policies. Women target women." WBI also found that there is strong public support for a Healthy Workplace Bill (HWB). "The strongest support comes from groups which enjoy protected status under current civil rights laws. Support from African Americans (73%) and Hispanics (66%) shows that current laws are inadequate when workplace cruelty is the issue. In fact, in 2009 the NAACP endorsed HWB as a necessary law."[32]

Notes

1. Abbey Payne, "Students Speak Out on Bullying," *Standard-Examiner* (Texas), May 29, 2012, www.standard.net/stories/2012/05/29/students-speak-out-bullying (accessed June 9, 2012).

2. Russell Goldman, "Teens Indicted after Allegedly Taunting Girl Who Hanged Herself," *ABC News*, March 29, 2010, abcnews.go.com/Technology/TheLaw/teens-charged-bullying-mass-girl-kill/story?id=10231357#.T2icNNnF9ac (accessed March 20, 2012).

3. Cameron Langford, "School Official Faces Suit on Bullied Teen's Suicide," *Courthouse News Service*, February 23, 2012, www.courthousenews.com/2012/02/23/44134.htm (accessed March 25, 2012).

4. Lara Glaswand, "Ginger Abuse: Tackling Redhead Harassment," *ABC News*, February 21, 2011, abcnews.go.com/WhatWouldYouDo/ginger-abuse-witnessed-discrimination-redhead/story?id=12929946 (accessed March 22, 2012).

5. Amelia, quoted in StudentsSpeakOut.org, "Students Speak Out Addresses Bullying in the 'School Safety' Discussion Group," Citizens League, June 6, 2008, www.citizing.org/data/pdfs/sso/SSOIssueBrief_Bullying.pdf (accessed March 24, 2012).

6. Annie, quoted in StudentsSpeakOut.org, "Students Speak Out Addresses Bullying in the 'School Safety' Discussion Group," Citizens League, June 6, 2008, www.citizing.org/data/pdfs/sso/SSOIssueBrief_Bullying.pdf (accessed March 24, 2012).

7. Sara Gartman, "Zach Veach, 17-Year-Old Race Car Driver Takes Down Competition and Bullies," *Huffington Post*, January 14, 2012, www.huffingtonpost.com/2012/01/12/zach-veach-teen-race-car-_n_1202420.html (accessed April 2, 2012).

8. Anju Kaur, "Sikhs at White House Conference on Bullying," *SikhNN*, March 20, 2011, www.sikhnn.com/headlines/1320/sikhs-white-house-conference-bullying (accessed August 26, 2012).

9. Kaur, "Sikhs at White House Conference on Bullying."

10. Fat-Freedom Fighter, quoted in "School," I Was a Fat Kid . . . This Is My Story, n.d., www.catay.com/fatkid/school.asp, n.d. (accessed March 22, 2012).

11. R. M. Puhl, T. Andreyeva, and K. D. Brownell, "Perceptions of Weight Discrimination: Prevalence and Comparison to Race and Gender Discrimination in America" (abstract), *International Journal of Obesity*, March 4, 2008, www.nature.com/ijo/journal/vaop/nncurrent/abs/ijo200822a.html (accessed March 22, 2012).

12. "Overweight Women More Likely Than Men to Face Weight Discrimination on Job," *Nation's Restaurant News*, November 12, 2007, 20.

13. Michael Buchanan and Diane Lang, *The Fat Boy Chronicles* (Ann Arbor, MI: Sleeping Bear Press, 2010), 54.

14. Buchanan and Lang, *The Fat Boy Chronicles*, 77.

15. Rachel Simmons, ed., *Odd Girl Speaks Out: Girls Write about Bullies, Cliques, Popularity, and Jealousy* (Orlando: Harcourt, 2004), 112–13.

16. Simmons, *Odd Girl Speaks Out*, 125.

17. Simmons, *Odd Girl Speaks Out*, viii.

18. Stephanie Newman, "Does Technology Harm Teen Relationships?" *Psychology Today*, January 16, 2012, www.psychologytoday.com/print/85181 (accessed May 31, 2012).

19. See www.bullying.org/external/documents/ACF19B6.pdf; also see www.stopbullying.gov/topics/what_is_bullying/test_your_knowledge/index.html and www.abc2news.com/dpp/news/education/no_2_bullying/biggest-facts-and-myths-about-bullying (accessed March 21, 2012).

20. National Crime Prevention Council, "Stop Cyberbullying before It Starts," n.d., www.ncpc.org/resources/files/pdf/bullying/cyberbullying.pdf (accessed March 25, 2012).

21. Maggie Flick, "Some Cyber Bullies Like to Hide behind the Impersonal Nature of the Web," *blog.mlive.com*, February 1, 2012, blog.mlive.com/citpat/news_impact/print.html?entry=/2012/02/some_cyber_bullies_like_to_hid.html (accessed March 25, 2012).

22. Quoted from *AskReddit* (blog), March 14, 2012, www.reddit.com/r/AskReddit/comments/qvgi5/the_cyber_bullying_has_gotten_to_the_point_where/ (accessed March 31, 2012).

23. Quoted from *AskReddit* (blog).

24. Eileen Fitzgerald, "Ridgefield High School Students Fight Bullying Tweets," *CTPost.com*, January 31, 2012, www.ctpost.com/local/article/Ridgefield-High-students-fight-bullying-tweets-2888097.php (accessed April 3, 2012).

25. National Conference of State Legislatures, "State Cyberstalking and Cyberharassment Laws," last updated March 23, 2012, www.ncsl.org/issues-research/telecom/cyberstalking-and-cyberharassment-laws.aspx (accessed March 31, 2012).

26. Robyn Moltzen, "Everyday Law: New Bullying Laws in California," *Sacramento Press*, February 1, 2012, www.sacramentopress.com/headline/63047/Everyday_Law_New_Bullying_Laws_in_California (accessed March 31, 2012).

27. U.S. Department of Education, Office of Civil Rights, *Sexual Harassment: It's Not Academic* (Washington, D.C.: Author, 2008), 3.

28. The Nemours Foundation/KidsHealth, "Sexual Harassment and Sexual Bullying," Teens Health, reviewed August 2011, kidshealth.org/teen/sexual_health/guys/harassment.html (accessed December 7, 2012).

29. Catherine Hill and Holly Kearl, *Crossing the Line: Sexual Harassment at School* (Washington, D.C.: American Association of University Women, 2011), 2; available online at www.aauw.org/learn/research/upload/CrossingTheLine.pdf (accessed March 31, 2012).

30. Bullying Statistics, "Workplace Bullying," n.d., www.bullyingstatistics.org/content/workplace-bullying.html (accessed April 2, 2012).

31. Marlow Stern, "How Katy Butler, 'Bully' Documentary's Teen Crusader, Was Bullied," *Daily Beast*, March 28, 2012, www.thedailybeast.com/articles/2012/03/28/how-katy-butler-bully-documentary-s-teen-crusader-was-bullied.html (accessed April 1, 2012).

32. Workplace Bullying Institute, "Results of the 2010 and 2007 WBI U.S. Workplace Bullying Survey," 2010, www.workplacebullying.org/wbiresearch/2010-wbi-national-survey/ (accessed April 2, 2012).

BIGOTRY AND RACISM: STILL ALIVE AND WELL

··

"You never know what's going to happen after school. . . .
'Cause I'm from Africa . . . [guys] always make fun of me. . . .
Just racist jokes. It's both races, white and black. It makes me feel sad."
—Fifteen-year-old Victor Uchendu of St. Petersburg, Florida[1]

Although many Americans believe that bigotry and racism are no longer part of U.S. society, that is hardly the case. Students at Monessen High School in Monessen, Pennsylvania, can attest to that fact. In February 2012, the school's basketball team, a black and biracial squad, was at the predominately white Brentwood High School in Pittsburgh for a game. The Monessen team won 59–45, but not before the Brentwood students tried to provoke the visiting team with taunts of "cotton pickers," "gorillas," and "monkeys." In addition, some fans paraded around in banana suits, which has a racist connotation—suggesting that the opposition players were banana lovers like monkeys.

Chavis Rawlins, one of the Monessen players, told *CBS News* that similar incidents had happened many times before. Another player, Justin Rawlins, told a reporter that the harassment, which included banana-suited students with monkey posters, "made me angry, but I just don't understand racism nowadays because from what I learned in school, it's from the past."[2]

However, the past was in the here and now in the town of Tonawanda near Buffalo, New York, in December 2011. The Kenmore East High School girls' varsity basketball team had a pregame routine. When adults left the locker room, the girls would "hold hands before their games, say a prayer together, then yell 'One, two, three, [N word],' before running out onto the court," according to a news report. The chant was used often, even though one of the Kenmore players, Tyra, is an African American. Tyra objected to the chant, but she was told by her teammates that "it's a tradition." Reporter Sandra Tan wrote, "Tyra added that her teammates would routinely make racial references and jokes during practice, including ones regarding slavery, shackles and 'picking cotton.'" Because of the racial slurs, Tyra attacked one of the players and both were suspended for getting into a fight. But once school officials investigated the cause of the incident, disciplinary actions were taken against other players. These included a two-day suspension for the players who took part in the chant, cancellation of a team field trip, sensitivity training, and forfeit of a sportsmanship award.[3]

In Florida, two white students at Gainesville High School produced a racist video that was posted on YouTube on a Tuesday in February 2012. By Thursday, the video had been posted on other sites and was seen by hundreds of thousands of viewers. The video included the girls' ugly comments about black people, such as black people can't speak right and most blacks are on welfare and use their money to buy iPhones and other gadgets but can't buy good food. And "most of the crime here [in Gainesville] is done by black people." And "there are black people . . . and there are niggers. And there's a difference." The girls, whose names were not reported because they are minors, continued their insulting and offensive comments.[4]

Because of threats against the girls and their families, their parents withdrew the girls from Gainesville High School. The girls themselves issued apologies and insisted they were not racists, but were responding to "alleged hate mail" apparently sent by black students. According to the *Gainesville Sun*, "The family hopes the community can heal, forgive and move forward." One of the girls told the *Sun*'s reporter "I'm not a racist person. I still don't see someone and judge them because of skin color, [but after the video], no one is going to believe me anymore."[5]

The same month (February 2012) two giggling white girls at Santaluces High School in Palm Beach County, Florida, produced their own racist video, making fun of black students, the way they talk and walk and the black girls' weaves. During the four-minute video, one of the girls brushes her long, dark hair, while the other flips her blonde tresses aside and rolls her eyes.[6] YouTube removed the video twice, calling it a violation of their policy banning hate speech. But the video surfaced on Facebook pages and school officials have had to deal with the negative fallout. It was not certain whether the girls would face hate crime charges.

YouTube was the site for another racist video with two teenage girls in Arizona spewing a rant against Mexican immigrants in January 2012. In this six-minute video, the girls talk about how "nasty and raunchy" Mexicans are and almost every sentence includes expletives, for example, telling immigrants, "Grab your burritos and get the fuck out of our country." But as Ashley Cardiff noted in her post at thegloss.com/culture/racist-video-arizona-girls-mexican-immigrants-773/, those comments are mild compared to the rest of the video. The video was taken down not long after it appeared but it reemerged on other

What Some Black Male Teens Say

The *Tampa Bay Times* interviewed about a dozen black teenagers in Florida's Tampa Bay area in April 2012, asking the teens about racism, how they see themselves, what their experiences have been, and what their values are. Here are a few comments that appeared in print and on a video:

"I'm not just a black male teen. I'm a human being. . . . I'm an educated person."—Fifteen-year-old Alex Harris of Tampa

"Not all black people are the same. . . . Since I was a kid, you give respect and you earn it."—Eighteen-year-old Casey Clement of St. Petersburg

"I have the same rights as everyone else. . . . I think I should be a leader, not a follower. I do a lot of volunteer work."—Sixteen-year-old Cedric Whitley of Tampa

"I felt threatened when I was walking by myself and I had my phone out and there was like a big group of people just walking towards me. . . . I put my phone back in my pocket nonchalantly and then just kept on walking. . . . They didn't bother me because I didn't bother them."—Seventeen-year-old Leon Tomlinson of St. Petersburg[7]

websites, and Cardiff included it in her post, which could still be accessed as of September 1, 2012. The Phoenix police said they would not prosecute the girls because no matter how repulsive their comments, they are protected under the First Amendment.

Beyond the School Campus

High school students, of course, are not the only people who display their bigotry and racism. Racism is evident in the military, for example. Consider the case of Danny Chen, a nineteen-year-old U.S. soldier. In August 2011 he was sent to a

U.S. Army post in Afghanistan. He died there in October 2011, not from combat but by his own hand. He shot himself after being repeatedly harassed by a superior officer and seven other soldiers who heckled and attacked Chen because of his Chinese ancestry.

From the time he first arrived in Afghanistan, "a group of his superiors allegedly tormented Chen on an almost daily basis. . . . They singled him out, their only Chinese-American soldier, and spit racial slurs at him: 'gook,' 'chink,' 'dragon lady,'" according to a feature story in *New York Magazine*. The officers "forced [Chen] to do sprints while carrying a sandbag. They ordered him to crawl along gravel-covered ground while they flung rocks at him. And one day, when his unit was assembling a tent, he was forced to wear a green hard-hat and shout out instructions to his fellow soldiers in Chinese."[8] The eight were charged with dereliction of duty and assault and endangerment, and each faced a court-martial, or military court.

At his court-martial in mid-2012, Sergeant Adam Holcomb, one of the officers who harassed Chen, was found guilty of assault and maltreatment of Chen and was sentenced to thirty days in jail. His rank was reduced from sergeant to specialist, his pay was cut, and he also was fined $1,181.55. The other seven soldiers charged in Chen's death also faced their courts-martial. One of the soldiers, Specialist Ryan J. Offutt, was sentenced in August 2012. He was reduced "in rank to E-1, confinement for 6 months and a bad conduct discharge for hazing and maltreating Pvt. Danny Chen in Afghanistan," according to a report by Kelly Twedell on *Fort Bragg Patch*.[9] Staff Sergeant Blaine G. Dugas Jr. also was sentenced in August. He was demoted to sergeant but was not sentenced to any time in prison. The other soldiers were scheduled for court-martial in late October and early November 2012.

Another soldier, Army Specialist Brushaun Anderson, was also subjected to harassment and racist torment by his superior officers in a remote base in eastern Baghdad, Iraq. Anderson was one of only a few black soldiers in his 2-15 Field Artillery Battalion. The newspaper *Stars and Stripes*, which reports on U.S. military matters and operates within the U.S. Department of Defense, published his story, describing how "senior noncommissioned officers" ruled Anderson's life. He was ordered "to wear a plastic trash bag because they said he was 'dirty.'" Repeatedly Anderson was forced "to perform excessive physical exercises in his body armor." His superiors "made him build a sandbag wall that served no military purpose." Noted the newspaper feature:

Anderson seemed to take it all in stride. Until New Year's Day 2010, when the once-eager 20-year-old soldier locked himself inside a portable toilet, picked up his M4 rifle, aimed the barrel at his forehead and pulled the trigger.

Anderson left behind a note lamenting his failures in the military, and some soldiers in his unit immediately said that Anderson had been driven to kill himself by leaders bent on humiliating him.

"No matter what Spc. Anderson did, no matter how big or small the incident was, his punishment was always extremely harsh, [and] a lot of the time demeaning," one corporal later told Army investigators.

"Spc. Anderson's punishments were not like anyone else's in the platoon," another corporal said. "Spc. Anderson was singled out."[10]

Army investigators found that officers in the 2-15 Field Artillery Battalion, treated soldiers, "Anderson in particular . . . in a cruel, abusive, oppressive and harmful manner." However, the officers were not disciplined and remained in the army.[11]

In the civilian world, racism and bigotry are still evident in numerous places: on the Internet; in the streets; in politics; in housing developments; in the

See This Flick: The Help

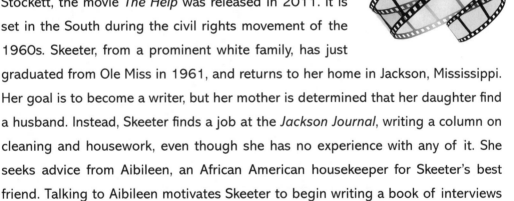

Based on an award-winning 2009 novel by Kathryn Stockett, the movie *The Help* was released in 2011. It is set in the South during the civil rights movement of the 1960s. Skeeter, from a prominent white family, has just graduated from Ole Miss in 1961, and returns to her home in Jackson, Mississippi. Her goal is to become a writer, but her mother is determined that her daughter find a husband. Instead, Skeeter finds a job at the *Jackson Journal*, writing a column on cleaning and housework, even though she has no experience with any of it. She seeks advice from Aibileen, an African American housekeeper for Skeeter's best friend. Talking to Aibileen motivates Skeeter to begin writing a book of interviews with the maids of Jackson. But that is a dangerous mission since the black women could lose their jobs if the project becomes known.

The real story of *The Help* is about the lives of Jackson's maids and caretakers, told from their point of view. Aibileen, played by Viola Davis, who won an academy award for best supporting actress, is the first to discuss her life and eventually others take part, telling their stories. As portrayed in the movie, the women's lives are an accurate depiction of the kind of denigrating treatment black domestic servants endured during the 1950s and 1960s.

For many Americans the Confederate (or rebel) flag represents racism and bigotry, although some view it as a symbol of southern pride.

workplace; in places of worship. Take a look at the Internet and using a browser type in the question, Is racism alive and well in America? About twenty million sites will appear. Some are duplicates, but the content of numerous postings tell of people who have experienced racism and bigotry in the here and now. They tell of casual conversations in which people say quite emphatically in public "I hate niggers" or "People who want gun control laws are bigots" or "Burning the Koran is allowed under the U.S. Constitution" or "Today's sermon is the Cult of Mormonism."

How Bigotry and Racism Are Sustained

No one begins life with bigoted and racist attitudes, but a variety of factors help sustain bigotry and racism throughout one's lifetime. In many cases, family members can influence what people believe about those who appear different from their relatives and friends. That is often the case when parents make bigoted remarks about homosexuals or use racist terms to describe people of color. In the *Washington Times*, Jamie Tankersley tells of her experiences with embedded racism (defined as "subliminal racism"):

> Growing up in an all-white neighborhood had its blessings and curses, but one of the most vile blights in my early life was having racial dogma imprinted in my heart.
>
> These teachings were passed down to me by family, friends and neighbors, who were either unaware or fully conscious of their bigotry. Nevertheless, their daily indulgence in white separatism, intolerant jokes and confederate loyalty encouraged me to become a teenage racist.
>
> My personal encounter with racial intolerance occurred in high school where I met a fellow student who was not white. My immediate thought was to avoid him because he is not like me; in fact it was very difficult to say hello because no true southerner would be caught dead talking to a black person because fraternizing with someone inferior was forbidden, distasteful and considered a betrayal of one's own race. These thoughts lingered for weeks as I wrestled with both my conscious and my traditions. I knew I was wrong, but in my mind I wanted to be part of my country's southern heritage. But as time went forth Providence, personal association and time enlightened me to the immorality and foolishness of my upbringing.[12]

Because it is common for many Caucasian children to be brought up in neighborhoods with few or no people of diverse heritage and religions, they may learn at an early age that some groups are "unacceptable." Parents or other adults might warn a child not to play with "those people." However the term *those people* is usually replaced with racial or ethnic slurs such as *spics*, *gooks*, *greasy wops*, *kikes*, *desert niggers*, or any number of other offensive labels too numerous and not worth the space to list. The adults' words may be reinforced with facial expressions and gestures that clearly imply that it is repugnant to associate with those thought to be inferior.

Another way that bigotry and racism are sustained is by stereotyping—judging a stranger by the color of his or her skin and/or attire. The Trayvon Martin case is an example. Seventeen-year-old Trayvon Martin, a black youth, was killed by a member of a neighborhood watch group, George Zimmerman, who is Hispanic. Martin was in a gated community in Sanford, Florida, where his father was visiting; the teenager was returning from a convenience store with a can of ice tea and a bag of candy. It was raining, and he was wearing a hoodie and talking on his cell phone. Zimmerman followed Martin, allegedly because the teenager was a stranger in the community and looked "suspicious."

Martin confronted Zimmerman, apparently asking why he was being followed. A fight ensued and Martin was shot dead. Zimmerman was charged with second-degree murder but his lawyer claimed self-defense under the highly controversial stand-your-ground law, which says a person who fears great bodily harm has no duty to retreat and may respond with deadly force. The law, however, does not allow someone to invoke stand-your-ground if he or she initiated a confrontation or deliberately put himself or herself in harm's way.

Economic and political considerations are major factors in continued racism and bigotry. Racism persists in order to maintain the status quo, or the social structure that now exists. In the United States, members of the white male majority hold most of the political power and also control most of the large corporations and businesses. It is not likely that people within that power structure will voluntarily give up their advantages and privileged positions. As a result, when others try to gain power through economic influence or political office, they are seen as threats and some members of the power structure may then try to combat that threat by denying "outsiders" opportunities for advancement.

If people do not advance financially or become unemployed, they often are stereotyped with bigoted labels. The financially stable may suggest that the unemployed and poor are "just plain lazy," "don't want to do for themselves," or "prefer to take a government handout rather than work." The assumption is that people have brought financial problems on themselves. However, as was clear during the great recession or the global financial crisis that took hold in the late 2000s, jobs were scarce across the United States and in other countries. Large financial institutions collapsed, the housing market fell and homes were worth much less than their original cost, people lost their homes to foreclosure, and businesses

Does a hoodie make someone look as though he will cause harm? Many youth and adults wear hooded sweatshirts like the one depicted here because they are comfortable, protective apparel.

closed because consumers could not afford their goods or services. In short, many victims of the financial crisis have not been responsible for their losses.

Racism and bigotry also can be seen in the information technology (IT) field. According to a 2011 report entitled *The Tilted Playing Field: Hidden Bias in Information Technology Workplaces*, there are unequal opportunities for women and people of color. The report is based on data collected from companies in the San Francisco (California) Bay area. It reveals that women and people of color encounter negative workplace experiences such as being unable to balance work and family, being excluded from some groups, and for women, being victims of bullying. In addition, the report points out,

> Experimental research . . . has demonstrated subtle yet significant biases against applicants with ethnic-sounding names, accents, and affiliation with LGBT organizations, where these individuals were perceived as less qualified during interviews and were less likely to receive "call-backs" from resumes than their non-negatively stigmatized peers. Despite organizational processes that appear to be impartial (e.g., merit pay), research demonstrates that biases exist in the performance rewards process where women and people of color receive lower pay for the same level of performance in comparison to white males.[13]

Bigotry and Racism in the Media

Over the years blatant racist materials have appeared in diverse forms and media in the United States. One negative image that was kept alive for many years was the view of the black male as a Sambo character. The black man was singled out to be the buffoon, with oversized lips lined with red, bulging eyes, always grinning broadly, dancing, singing, joking—or more frequently being the butt of jokes—looking and acting foolish for the entertainment of white folks. Such an image was rooted in slavery when black men, women, and children were expected to sing and dance as well as work for the white slave masters. After slavery was abolished, the male Sambo character appeared in a great variety of products such as post cards, children's games and books, playing cards, sheet music covers, food packages, placemats, pillows, goblets, and tea sets. The Sambo figure also was part of skits, musicals, circuses, radio and TV shows, and even in parades. And countless Sambo-type iron jockeys were planted on lawns or at driveway gates and they can still be seen in some areas of the United States.

Bigoted images that have had a long life in American culture include Jewish caricatures, which have portrayed Jews as aggressive, greedy, money-grabbing people. Cartoon figures—male or female—were always shown with prominent noses, and the men were made to appear sly or scheming. The images reflected

Did You Know?

Sambo's is the name of a former corporate chain of more than one thousand restaurants that originated in Santa Barbara, California. The first Sambo's was founded in 1957 by Sam Battistone Sr. and Newell Bohnett, known as Bo. They chose to call their restaurant Sambo's, which was a combination of their two names. As part of their marketing strategy, the partners used graphics from the children's book *The Story of Little Black Sambo* by Scottish author and illustrator Helen Bannerman. Sambo, the boy in the current restaurant graphics, appears to be from India and wears an Indian style turban. That depiction is from a revised edition of Bannerman's book, which uses authentic Indian names Babaji, for the boy, and Mamaji and Dadajia for the parents.

In the original story, the parents, named Black Mumbo and Black Jumbo, buy their son colorful new clothes, shoes, and an umbrella, and Sambo takes a walk wearing his fine new attire. Along the way he encounters a series of tigers. Each tiger threatens to eat the boy unless he gives up a piece of his clothing, and finally even his umbrella. The tigers return, arguing over who is the grandest animal and chasing each other around a tree. They race so fast that they turn into butter, which the boy takes home to use on the pancakes his mother makes.

While the revised version of *Little Black Sambo* shows a light-skinned family, the art for the original book depicts a caricature of a young boy with ink-black skin, large red mouth, and popping eyes, and he resembles the stereotyped plantation "darky." The same is true of the parents. That version can be seen online at www.sterlingtimes.co.uk/sambo.htm and also at archive.org/details/storyoflittleblabanner.

During the civil rights era of the 1960s and 1970s, the Sambo name was widely condemned as a deeply offensive racist term for African Americans and protests erupted. Some restaurants tried changing their names, but in the 1980s the restaurants began to fail and the corporation declared bankruptcy. Now, only the original restaurant remains near the beach in Santa Barbara.

the Anglo dislike (and sometimes hatred) of Jews, whom they believed were responsible for the death of Christ. In addition, the majority of Americans viewed Jews as an alien "race" and resented Jewish immigrants who managed to rise from rags to riches through menial labor and careful money management; their financial success was attributed to haggling and greed. Yet when other groups acquired wealth, the earnings were credited to hard work and thrift.

Long before the 2001 al-Qaeda attacks on the United States, negative images of Arabs permeated the American culture, because even though the U.S. Census Bureau categorizes Arabs as white, there is a perception among some Americans that Arabs are not quite white and thus must be evildoers. For many years, cartoons, comic strips, illustrations in children's books, and even Halloween costumes presented Arabs with huge noses and other features considered unfavorable. Arabs were portrayed as arrogant, rich oil sheiks, menacing villains, and greedy characters.

Bigoted and racist putdowns of indigenous people have persisted ever since the first European explorers set foot on the American continent. Tribal groups have been presented as warlike, uncivilized, alcoholics, lazy, and always living off the government. The labels ignore the fact that the federal governments of both the United States and Canada historically have been responsible for the loss of Indian lands, placing tribes on reservations, and forcing dependency by isolating them from the rest of society.

In addition, stereotypes of indigenous people have been commonplace in toys, films, textbooks, and countless other items sold in the United States. And there are baseball teams with names like Atlanta Braves, Cleveland Indians, Edmonton Eskimos, and Florida State Seminoles, and the Washington, D.C., football team called the Redskins. Jack Shakely, former chairman of the Los Angeles City/County Native American Indian Commission, asks, "In 21st century America, to name a sports team after an African American, Asian or any other ethnic group is unthinkable. So why are Native Americans still fair game?" Good question.[14]

John Two-Hawks on *Native Circle* website explains how Redsk**s, as he presents the term, is equivalent to using the N word to name a team. He writes,

Used as a name for many sports teams, this word is offensive by its very nature. In it's [*sic*] origin, it refers to the bloody scalps of Indian children, women and men that were sold for bounties aside animal skins in the USA. At this sad period in American history, Indians young and old, male and female, were hunted like animals by bounty hunters. They were killed, and then scalped. When these bounty hunters would come to the trading post, they would receive payment for their deer-skins, their beaver-skins, their raccoon-skins, and their *red*-skins. It is sickening that this horrifying word is still used as a sports team name.[15]

Being subjected to bigotry and racism is nothing new for people of Asian ancestry in America. Frequently they have been accused of taking jobs away from native-born Americans. In recent times, the emphasis has been on U.S. connections with China. A senatorial candidate from Michigan, Pete Hoekstra, ran a 2012 commercial in which an actress played the role of a Chinese woman riding her bike near a rice paddy supposedly in China. In the ad she said, "Your [U.S.] economy get very weak. Ours get very good. We take your jobs." After a public outcry against the ad, which was filmed in California, it was removed. The actress Lisa Chan of the San Francisco Bay area later apologized on Facebook:

> I am deeply sorry for any pain that the character I portrayed brought to my communities. As a recent college grad who has spent time working to improve communities and empower those without a voice, this role is not in any way representative of who I am. It was absolutely a mistake on my part and one that, over time, I hope can be forgiven. I feel horrible about my participation and I am determined to resolve my actions.[16]

New York Knicks point guard Jeremy Lin, the son of Taiwanese immigrants, knows about racism first hand. He has been called Chink, sweet-and-sour pork, and other racist names when he is on the court. "It's everything you can imagine," he told a reporter. "Racial slurs, racial jokes, all having to do with being Asian." Even when he played at Harvard from 2006 to 2010 he was taunted while at Ivy League gyms. Lin noted that he heard the slurs "at most of the Ivies if not all of them."[17]

While racial and bigoted slurs often occur during team sports events, some of the most vociferous forms of bigotry and racism in current times are the comments on talk shows, social networking sites like Facebook, and in the political arena. Increasingly, people take sides in terms of declaring who or who is not a bigot and who or who is not a racist. For example, people who are opposed to same-sex marriage are called bigots by proponents of same-sex unions. Supporters of immigration reform declare that anti-immigration folks are racists. In many instances, people participate in a war of words, symbols, and graphics to deliver their messages; they engage in the language of bigotry and racism.

Notes

1. Joseph Garnett Jr., "Young. Black. Male.," *Tampa Bay Times*, Perspective section, April 15, 2012, 1.
2. Brenda Waters, "Brentwood HS Officials Investigate Racial Slur Claims," *CBS Pittsburgh*, February 8, 2012, pittsburgh.cbslocal.com/2012/02/08/brentwood-hs-officials-investigate -racial-slur-claims/ (accessed February 15, 2012).

3. Sandra Tan, "Basketball Players Suspended for N-Word," *BuffaloNews.com*, December 9, 2011, www.buffalonews.com/city/communities/tonawanda/article665195.ece (accessed February 16, 2011). See also Adam S. Levy, "11 Members of Girls High School Basketball Team Suspended for N-Word Chant," RadarOnline.com, www.radaronline.com/exclusives/2011/12/tyra-batts-buffalo-basketball-n-word-racism (accessed December 10, 2012).

4. *Racist White Teen Girl Goes on a Rant about Blacks* (video), richardemanuel.wordpress.com/2012/02/23/racist-white-teen-girl-goes-on-a-rant-about-blacks-then-the-shit-hits-the-fan/ (accessed December 10, 2012).

5. Jackie Alexander, "Families of Girls in Racist Videos Express Remorse," *Gainesville.com*, February 20, 2012, scene.gainesville.com/article/20120220/ARTICLES/120229958/0/PREPS (accessed April 7, 2012)

6. Allison Ross, "Racist Video by Two Santaluces High Girls Leads to Extra Security at School," *Palm Beach Post*, updated February 23, 2012, www.palmbeachpost.com/news/news/education/racist-video-by-two-santaluces-high-girls-leads-to/nL4Hr/ (accessed December 10, 2012).

7. Garnett, "Young. Black. Male.," 1.

8. Jennifer Gonnerman, "Pvt. Danny Chen, 1992–2011," *New York Magazine*, January 6, 2012, nymag.com/news/features/danny-chen-2012-1/ (accessed April 12, 2012).

9. Kelly Twedell, "Second Soldier Convicted in Court-Martial Case of Pvt. Danny Chen's Death," *Fort Bragg Patch*, August 13, 2012, fortbragg.patch.com/articles/second-soldier-in-court-martial-case-of-pvt-danny-chen-s-death-charged (accessed October 5, 2012).

10. Megan McCloskey, "One Army, Two Failures," *Stars and Stripes*, June 7, 2011, www.stripes.com/news/special-reports/suicide-in-the-military/maltreated-and-hazed-one-soldier-is-driven-to-take-his-own-life-1.145941 (accessed April 13, 2012).

11. "AR-15-16 Investigation—Corrective Training and Improper Punishment within 2-15 Field Artillery Battalion," www.stripes.com/polopoly_fs/1.146076!/menu/standard/file/3anderson_report.pdf (accessed April 13, 2012).

12. Shirley Husar, "Do You Suffer from Embedded Racism?" *Washington Times*, March 25, 2012, communities.washingtontimes.com/neighborhood/urban-game-changer/2012/mar/25/obama-ignites-embedded-racism-campaign-trail/ (accessed April 8, 2012).

13. Level Playing Field Institute, *The Tilted Playing Field: Hidden Bias in Information Technology Workplaces*, September 2011, www.lpfi.org/sites/default/files/tilted_playing_field_lpfi_9_29_11.pdf (accessed April 9, 2012).

14. Jack Shakely, "Indian Mascots—You're Out," *Los Angeles Times*, August 25, 2011, articles.latimes.com/print/2011/aug/25/opinion/la-oe-shakely-teams-20110825 (accessed April 15, 2012).

15. John Two-Hawks, "How 'Indian' Mascots Oppress," Native Circle, n.d., www.nativecircle.com/mascots.htm (accessed April 15, 2012).

16. Amy Bingham, "Actress in 'Offensive' Pete Hoekstra Ad Apologizes, Calls Ad a 'Mistake,'" *ABC News*, February 16, 2012, abcnews.go.com/blogs/politics/2012/02/actress-in-offensive-pete-hoekstra-ad-apologizes-calls-ad-a-mistake/ (accessed April 24, 2012). Also see David Catanese, "Actress in Hoekstra Ad Apologizes," *Politico*, February 15, 2012, www.politico.com/blogs/david-catanese/2012/02/actress-in-hoekstra-ad-apologizes-114643.html (accessed April 24, 2012).

17. Sean Gregory, "Harvard's Hoops Star Is Asian: Why's That a Problem?" *Time*, December 31, 2009, www.time.com/time/printout/0,8816,1953708,00.html (accessed April 24, 2012).

THE LANGUAGE OF BIGOTRY AND RACISM

"Derogatory terms are a common form of racism that highlights cultural differences.
. . . Those who use racial slurs are obviously misguided, and feeding their insults
with a reply does nothing but promote further prejudice. Lacking a response,
racists don't receive the negative attention (and achieve the intentional offense)
they seek. I believe that over time, these reprobates will stop using derogatory
terms, thus eliminating xenophobic language from common use."
—*Kari S. of Tiburon, California, writing in* Teen Ink[1]

One of the most powerful forces in keeping bigotry and racism alive is language—words and symbols and how they are used. Words shape thought; they can be used as propaganda and to spread opinions or beliefs. Words can intimidate or be direct threats of violence. So can symbols. Words and symbols can reinforce stereotypes and perpetuate racism and bigotry.

A look at some history books provides some examples, such as the use of "loaded" words to distort conquests of indigenous people. If whites won battles, they were called victories; if Native Americans won battles, they were called massacres by savages, rather than, say, battles to defend their homelands.

Many old sayings are based on bigoted notions. Consider the stereotyped image of Jews as "cheap" and always ready to bargain or cheat others. That stereotype is reflected in the derogatory saying "Jewing down," meaning getting the price down. Or a stereotyped saying might be "Drunk as an Irishman" or "Teenagers are punks" or "British people are snobs" or "Polacks are stupid" or "Cubans are loud" or dozens if not hundreds of other statements denigrating an entire group of people.

The English language itself is sometimes a tool to keep bigotry and racism alive. There has been a long-standing controversy in the United States and often a heated debate over whether English should be the only language allowed in schools. Students have been reprimanded and punished for not speaking English. One U.S. high school student was stopped in her school hallway while she was speaking Spanish with a friend. "This is America," a group of schoolmates taunted. In other words, speak English—or else! Or as one bumper sticker put it, "Speak English—or Die!"

In September 2008, a North Carolina elementary school secretary, Ana Ligia Mateo, was reprimanded because she violated a school policy that required the faculty and staff to speak only English. According to news reports, a Spanish-speaking mother came to the school, crying hysterically because her seven-year-old son was sexually abused at the school. A U.S. citizen from Nicaragua, Mateo tried to translate for the parent, but was told by the principal, Suzanne Gimenez, to let the boy translate for his mother. But the mother did not understand what the school officials said and left the school without resolving the issue. Gimenez warned Mateo not to complain and accused the secretary of supporting Spanish-speaking parents because "she crossed the border just like them." Mateo continued to try to help Spanish-speaking parents and was fired. She filed a lawsuit in a state court in February 2010, charging the school district with violation of her civil rights. Since then, her case has been referred to the U.S. Justice Department. As for the young student, it is unknown whether anything was done to help him.

English-Only Policies

More than two dozen states have passed laws declaring English as the official language, and the English-only or English-first movement is campaigning to have the federal government legally establish English as the official language in the United States. The state laws are primarily symbolic, but across the United States, many people support the English-only ideas. For example, teenager Rishi A. wrote in *Teen Ink*,

> I believe our nation . . . should embrace English as the official language to ensure the future unity of our nation. Adopting the English language has been an integral part of becoming an "American." The English language serves as a national glue that not only binds, but also unites immigrants with native-born Americans. Although our love of freedom and democratic ideals help to unite and give Americans a sense of purpose, it is ultimately English which allows us to communicate with each other, discuss our views, and encourage trust, while reducing racial hostility and bigotry.[2]

Opponents say that proposals for adopting English as the official language include "the elimination of oral or written forms of bilingual government services, bilingual education, bilingual ballots, and bilingual citizenship tests. Government services include access to public safety services, health services, social welfare services, courtroom translation, and driver's license examinations," according to the National Asian Pacific American Legal Consortium. The Asian Pacific American Legal Center of Southern California notes that "for the 56% of the Asian Pacific population that is limited-English proficient, a declaration of English as the official language would deny access to health and safety services, the legal system, voting, education, and the workplace."[3]

The American Civil Liberties Union (ACLU) and other groups also have opposed English-Only laws. As the ACLU explained,

> The ACLU opposes "English Only" laws because they can abridge the rights of individuals who are not proficient in English, and because they perpetuate false stereotypes of immigrants and nonEnglish speakers. We believe, further, that such laws are contrary to the spirit of tolerance and diversity embodied in our Constitution. An English Language Amendment to the Constitution would transform that document from being a charter of liberties and individual freedom into a charter of restrictions that limits, rather than protects, individual rights.[4]

Others who are against English-only laws argue that such legislation stems from bigoted and racist attitudes toward immigrants, most of whom come from Asia and Spanish-speaking countries. A case in point: In Pahrump, Nevada, the town board voted 3–2 in 2006 to pass an ordinance that declared "English as the town's official language, set restrictions on flying foreign flags and denied town benefits to undocumented immigrants. Approval of the ordinance was met with a standing ovation and cheers by many of the approximately 250 people at the meeting. One man wore a stars and stripes bandana on his head and a T-shirt that said: Speak English or get the (expletive) out," noted a report in the *Las Vegas Review-Journal*.[5]

Sheriff Tony DeMeo refused to enforce the ordinance, and it was repealed within a few months, but at the time Andy Sanchez told a *Los Angeles Times* reporter Ashley Powers, "I didn't know that kind of racism was here. . . . It broke my heart." However, by the summer of 2011, Sanchez was encouraged by a group of local activists campaigning for the recall of Nye County Assessor Shirley Matson, "who compared Latinos to 'locusts,' said pregnant Latinas were carrying 'anchor babies' and told the sheriff she was fearful of 'Mexican/Latino, non-English speaking' construction workers building a nearby jail," according to Powers. The reporter noted that the recall efforts are partially due to the change in the state's population with about half consisting of Latinos.[6] On April 19, 2012, the Nevada Commission on Ethics found Matson guilty of ethics violations and fined her five thousand dollars. The commission also said Matson "failed to avoid conflicts between her private interests and those of the public, and used her position to intimidate, harass other officials and employees to defend against recall efforts. They also found by a 3–2 vote [that] Matson used government time, property, equipment or other facilities to benefit her personal or financial interest, in taping signs on her county vehicle," the *Pahrump Valley Times* reported. The commissioners chose not to remove Matson from office.[7]

Bigoted and Racist Signs and Symbols

Symbols and graphics often take the place of words to send bigoted or racist messages. Consider the insulting racist symbols that have appeared at sports events, such as the degrading mascots and "Indian" names and logos that have denigrated tribal Americans. One example has been the Cleveland Indians' logo of Chief Wahoo, who is depicted as a "leering, big-nosed, buck-toothed redskin caricature," as Jack Shakely, former chairman of the Los Angeles City/County Native American Indian Commission, described it. Another is Chief Noc-A-Homa, who was the original mascot of the Milwaukee, Wisconsin, and Atlanta Braves. The mascot, in Shakely's words, "came stomping and war-dancing his way out of a tepee in center field every time the Braves hit a home run. He was dressed in a Plains Indian chief's eagle bonnet and acted like a village idiot."[8] In 1986, the baseball team retired its mascot.

"Some symbols are meant to convey feelings of hate or anger, or meant to instill in those who see the symbols feelings of fear and insecurity," says the Anti-Defamation League (ADL). "Hate symbols, for instance, can be found scrawled on the outside walls of synagogues, churches and schools; tattooed on the bodies of white supremacists; or displayed on jewelry or clothing. These symbols give extremists a sense of power and belonging, as well as a quick way of identifying others who share their beliefs."[9]

Here is what a quick look at Internet and news stories about displays of racist symbols, bigotry, and intolerance revealed in 2012:

- Teenagers paint "White power!" graffiti on a wall.
- At Notre Dame University in Indiana, some students place fried chicken parts in the mailboxes of the Black Students Association and the African Students Association.
- Three teenage girls draw swastikas and place dog feces along with the word *Jew* on a sidewalk outside a Jewish home.
- An anti-Obama "joke" is passed via e-mail that features the image of a mother and son under the title "A Mother's Love." The e-mail reads, "A

little boy said to his mother, 'Mommy, how come I'm black and you're white?' His mother replied, 'Don't even go there, Barack! From what I can remember about that party, you're lucky you don't bark!'"

- Two sixteen-year-olds create a giant swastika out of twenty-eight folding chairs; they place in front of a synagogue in Long Island, New York.
- A racist anti–President Obama bumper sticker reads, "Don't Re-Nig in 2012" and below it says, "Stop repeat offender. Don't re-elect Obama!" A photograph of the bumper sticker was displayed on Facebook and quickly spread across the Internet. Two sites that included the offensive bumper sticker were shut down.
- An anti-Obama T-shirt reads, "Hold Your Nose 'Til 2013. America's Got B.O."
- A bumper sticker says, "Real Men Marry Women."
- A noose hangs on a tree near an African American home.

Symbols of the Klan

Perhaps no racist symbols of the past were as intimidating as the Ku Klux Klan's garb. Known as the KKK or simply the Klan, members wore white sheets and cone-shaped hats with masks over their faces, and they burned crosses in the yards and communities of African Americans. Since the end of the U.S. Civil War, the Klan has terrorized black people and also Jews, Catholics, immigrants, and women who fought for voting and other civil rights and job opportunities. While the KKK is still around and active in some parts of the United States, the group has lost much of its clout and power. Where once there were millions of members, the KKK now consists of about five to six thousand, thanks to civil rights laws and lawsuits that have brought an end to some groups or prompted members to join other racist organizations.

The Klan was one of the first terrorist groups in the United States, but contrary to popular belief it began rather innocently after the Civil War. Six veterans of the Confederacy formed a social club—a secret society—and gave themselves a Greek-sounding name, the Ghouls, and called their leaders by such titles as Grand Cyclops and Grand Magi. As a way to amuse themselves without revealing their identity, the new society members disguised themselves in sheets and rode on horseback through their little town of Pulaski, Tennessee. "Their ride created such a stir that the men decided to adopt the sheets as the official regalia of the Ku Klux Klan, and they added to the effect by donning grotesque masks and tall pointed hats," according to Klanwatch of the Southern Poverty Law Center.[10] Klanwatch was set up in 1980 to increase awareness of the KKK's violent nature and to provide legal help for victims of KKK terror tactics.

A noose frequently has been used symbolically as well as literally in lynchings to intimidate African Americans.

Membership in the Klan grew and after the Civil War night riders began to harass newly freed blacks. There was widespread fear that freed slaves would seek revenge or gain political control if allowed to vote and own property. So some Southern states adopted Black Codes, which denied blacks voting rights and property and restricted them to menial jobs. To further exercise white domination, Klan members began to turn to violent tactics, whipping, shooting, mutilating, and lynching innocent black people. Such terrorism continued unabated until the end of the 1860s when federal laws were passed to outlaw Klan activities.

The organization appeared to disband, but did not disappear. After the turn of the century the Klan revived, died out, and revived again a number of times. Over the years, many Klansmen and women have been consumed with hatred for people different from themselves, persecuting and killing male and female victims. Klan attacks against and murder of fellow humans frequently went on with the silent support of law officials and many community leaders.

After World War II, American society began to change somewhat as soldiers came home. Many black, Asian, Hispanic, and other groups began to organize to protest discriminatory and violent acts against minorities. At the same time, Congress passed civil rights laws and many civic leaders no longer tolerated the crimes of Klan members. Yet, from the mid-1950s through the 1980s, the Klan still operated, harassing, beating, and killing people of color.

By the 1990s, Klan membership was in decline once more, but its symbols have lived on. However, the white robes have been replaced with camouflage fatigues or black uniforms as Klan members join neo-Nazi or antigovernment militias intent on overthrowing the U.S. government. And they continue spewing their hatred of people of color, Jews, Muslims, and other minorities.

When a Mascot Looks Like a KKK Member

It happened in Ocala, Florida, in 2011. The KKK symbolic garb is still so potent that an advertiser wearing an ice cream cone costume was mistaken for a Klan member. An ice cream and sandwich shop hired Daniel Aviles to dress like an ice cream cone with a waffle-like cone shirt and a somewhat pointed white hood. Aviles stood on a corner in Ocala, carrying a sign advertising the shop and waving to potential customers. From a distance, the sign covered the cone part of the costume and the cone shaped top looked like a Klansman outfit. According to a news report, some people were so frightened that they refused to go near the shop or enter it. The owner told a reporter "One (customer) told me, 'I had to think twice before coming in here because I thought it was KKK.'"[11] Obviously, it was time for the ice cream cone to melt away!

Nazi Symbols

The swastika is the well-known symbol of German dictator Adolf Hitler's Nazi Party that was responsible for the death of millions of Jews plus Roma (called gypsies in English), handicapped people, and others considered "undesirable" in an extermination known as the Holocaust. During more recent history, the swastika and other symbols such as a skull and cross bones, a cross and white circle, and lightning bolts signifying the Schutzstaffel (or SS) German police force have been used by neo-Nazi groups to display their belief in white supremacy. Neo-Nazi groups worship Hitler and the views he espoused, among them the belief that Jews were in a conspiracy to destroy the Aryan race. Hitler declared that Aryans were born to rule because, in his view, they were superior to all other people. Hitler's ideas did not die with his death by suicide in 1945. His beliefs have been carried on by neo-Nazis.

Neo-Nazis organized in the United States during the 1960s and 1970s and to this day make no secret of their hatred for Jews, people of color, and homosexuals. Some groups wear symbolic uniforms that are designed to look like those of Hitler's, complete with the swastika armband and iron cross. The largest neo-Nazi group is the National Socialist Movement (NSM) with headquarters in Detroit, Michigan. Members wear "black fatigue-like clothing with NSM insignia. At rallies, the members, dressed in black pants and shirts, often carry banners or shields bearing the group's insignia, which includes a swastika and the NSM logo," according to the ADL.[12] One of its tenets clearly states its bigotry and racism: "Only those of pure White blood, whatever their creed, may be members of the nation. Non-citizens may live in America only as guests and must be subject to laws for aliens. Accordingly, no Jew or homosexual may be a member of the nation." Another says, "All non-White immigration must be prevented. We demand that all non-Whites currently residing in America be required to leave the nation forthwith and return to their land of origin: peacefully or by force."[13]

Other neo-Nazi groups still active include the American Nazi Party, Aryan Nations, racist skinheads, Stormfront, White Aryan Resistance, and dozens of others. The American Nazi Party symbol is a red flag with a swastika in the center; it's a variation of Hitler's Third Reich flag. Aryan Nations uses a blue shield with a sword topped by a crown. A black "death head" or skull symbolizes racist skinheads and neo-Nazi groups. Stormfront uses the words "White Pride World Wide" to surround a Celtic cross. The symbol for White Aryan Resistance is a skull with a black eye patch and cross bones underneath.

Some groups share the views of neo-Nazis but are not necessarily aligned with them. They include the Patriots, Christian Identity, and Sovereign Citizens. Patriots are opposed to what they call the New World Order and are antigovernment; some Patriot groups are armed militias whose guns and military-type training are

Adolf Hitler, shown with dictator Benito Mussolini, wears his swastika armband and the iron cross.

much more than symbols. These militias prepare to overthrow the U.S. government.

Christian Identity (or simply Identity) uses a gold crown as its symbol for a movement that clearly states its bigotry and racism. Identity's pseudo-Christian teachings are based on a "two-seed" theory of humankind's origin. In the biblical story of Adam and Eve, the couple had two sons—Cain and Abel—and out of jealousy Cain killed Abel. But according to Identity, the couple had two sons—Abel and Seth. Then Eve had sexual intercourse with Satan and produced Cain, who killed Abel. Seth's offspring supposedly make up the white race called the Lost Tribe of Israel, while Cain's descendants are Jews and blacks considered not fully human and without souls. It is the mission of the Christian Identity movement to rid the world of people who are not true Israelites.

Members of Sovereign Citizens include both white supremacists and black separatists who believe in ideas first espoused by Posse Comitatus, a Latin term for "power of the county." Followers of Posse Comitatus, which originated in 1969 in Portland, Oregon, believed they had a right to organize local governments with the sheriff as the top elected official. The sheriff was supposed to protect the people from other government officials (particularly federal and state officials), and if he did not he was subject to hanging. Thus the Posse symbols were a badge and a noose. Adopting Posse ideas, Sovereign Citizens groups defy federal and state government laws and "have engaged in a series of criminal acts, drawing up bogus financial instruments, harassing enemies with unjustified court filings, and

Did You Know?

The swastika was not always a symbol of intolerance, bigotry, and hate.

For thousands of years it was used by many cultures to convey a positive message of peace or good luck, or to express a religious view. Ancient Greeks used the symbol in architecture. It has long been an important symbol in India. The website Reclaim the Swastika says, "The swastika is to be seen everywhere across the Indian sub-continent: sculptured into temples both ancient and modern, decorating buildings, houses, shops, painted onto public buses, in taxis—even decorating the dashboards of the three-wheeler motor rickshaws. Many religious and spiritual books display the symbol. It may well be the most prevalent symbol one will see in India."[14]

For fifteen years members of the 45th Infantry Division of the U.S. Army wore swastika patches, considered a symbol of good luck by the division made up of indigenous soldiers. "The insignia served as recognition of the great number of Native Americans proudly serving in the 45th Infantry Division. The yellow swastika on a square background of red symbolized the Spanish Heritage of the 4 Southwestern states that made up the membership of the 45th—Oklahoma, New Mexico, Colorado, and Arizona." When the Nazi Party adopted the swastika, the 45th Division stopped using the symbol.[15]

even illegally seizing houses they do not own," notes the *Intelligence Report* of the Southern Poverty Law Center.[16]

Hate Music

Hate music is as much a part of bigoted and racist language as hateful speeches and graphics. Most Americans were unfamiliar with hate music until Wade Michael Page went on his murderous rampage and killed worshippers at a Wisconsin Sikh temple on August 5, 2012. As noted, Page was a member of a white power band, and news reports describing Page's involvement with white power and neo-Nazi music quickly appeared. Such bands have names that delineate their hatred: "Jew Slaughter, Grinded Nig, Angry Aryans, [and] Ethnic Cleansing. Page, a guitar player and singer, was once a member of 13 Knots, a name that refers to the number of knots in a noose," wrote Joe Heim in the *Washington Post*.[17]

White power bands have been performing in the United States since the late 1970s, according to Mark Pitcavage, director of ADL's investigative research. He writes,

> These bands and others like them are part of a thriving subculture; some white supremacists drive for hundreds of miles to attend their concerts. Their fans gather together, many sporting shaved heads and covered with tattoos. The men pump their fists in the air and dance raucously in front of a stage festooned with Nazi flags and racist skinhead symbols, while others, including a few women, watch around the perimeter. Onstage, the music is deafening, urging white people "to stand up and fight."[18]

The music, in fact, is "thunderous, thrashing heavy metal or punk music with lyrics that call for a race war," say Associated Press reporters Patrick Condon and Todd Richmond.[19] Between 100 and 150 white power bands perform in the United States at concerts and festivals; they also record on CDs and their music is available online.

When Hate Speech Is Protected

No matter how music and other forms of expression reflect hatred of certain groups, that hate language is protected. The Bill of Rights in the First Amendment to the U.S. Constitution, ratified by the states in 1791, declares, "Congress shall make no law respecting an establishment of religion, or prohibiting the free exercise thereof; or abridging the freedom of speech, or of the press; or the right of the people peaceably to assemble, and to petition the Government for a redress of grievances." The U.S. Courts' website explains what freedom of speech includes and does not include. For example, a person has the right *not* to speak as was determined in a case brought before the Supreme Court—*West Virginia Board of Education v. Barnette* (1943). The Court held that students cannot be compelled to salute the flag and as a form of free speech students have the freedom to refuse to do so.

In another case *Tinker v. Des Moines* (1969), which is often cited today, the Court determined that "students do not shed their constitutional rights at the school house gate" and can wear black armbands to school to protest a war. Americans also have the right to engage in symbolic speech such as burning the U.S. flag in a protest, which was determined in two Supreme Court decisions: *Texas v. Johnson* (1989) and *United States v. Eichman* (1990).

The U.S. Supreme Court has held that freedom of speech does not include the right to incite actions that would harm others such as the well-known example of shouting "fire" in a crowded theater that was determined in *Schenck v. United States* (1919); to make or distribute obscene materials (*Roth v. United States* [1957]); to burn draft cards as an antiwar protest (*United States v. O'Brien* [1968]); or to permit students to print articles in a school newspaper over the objections of the school administration (*Hazelwood School District v. Kuhlmeier* [1983]). Free speech rights do not protect students who make an obscene speech at a school-sponsored event (*Bethel School District #43 v. Fraser* [1986]), or students who advocate illegal drug use at a school-sponsored event (*Morse v. Frederick* [2007]).[20]

One of the most highly publicized and controversial instances of protected hate speech occurred in the 1970s when Nazi sympathizers (members of the Nationalist Social Party) planned to march in Skokie, Illinois, a Chicago suburb with a large Jewish population. Thousands were Holocaust survivors. Residents requested a court injunction against the march, and the village of Skokie denied permits for it. But the actions were declared unconstitutional—a violation of the First Amendment. Heated arguments and legal debates followed, and when the American Civil Liberties Union (ACLU) represented the Nazis, the organization lost numerous supporters. But "in the end, the Illinois Supreme Court, the United States Court of Appeals, and the United States Supreme Court contributed to the conclusion that Skokie could not enjoin the Nazis from marching," recalled Geoffrey Stone, who was a young law professor working with the ACLU at the time. Writing for the *Huffington Post*, Stone noted, "The outcome of the Skokie controversy was one of the truly great victories for the First Amendment in American history. It proved that the rule of law must and can prevail. Because of our profound commitment to the principle of free expression even in the excruciatingly painful circumstances of Skokie . . . we remain today the international symbol of free speech."[21]

Regarding recent instances of free speech appearing to go too far, consider the Topeka, Kansas, Westboro Baptist Church (WBC) members who have picketed hundreds of funerals of soldiers killed in action. The church consists of its leader, Fred Phelps, and immediate and extended family members, who believe that God hates the United States for its tolerance of homosexuality, particularly in America's military. At military funerals, WBC members wave posters that say, "Thank God for Dead Soldiers" and "Pray for More Dead Soldiers."

WBC members traveled to Maryland to picket the funeral of U.S. Marine Lance Corporal Matthew Snyder, who was killed in Iraq in the line of duty. Matthew Snyder's father filed a lawsuit that the U.S. Supreme Court argued in October 2010. Snyder charged that he suffered great emotional distress because of the picketing. But the Court ruled 8–1 in *Snyder v. Phelps* that the WBC speech was protected under the First Amendment, concluding,

Westboro's funeral picketing is certainly hurtful and its contribution to public discourse may be negligible. But Westboro addressed matters of public import on public property, in a peaceful manner, in full compliance with the guidance of local officials. The speech was indeed planned to coincide with Matthew Snyder's funeral, but did not itself disrupt that funeral, and Westboro's choice to conduct its picketing at that time and place did not alter the nature of its speech.

Speech is powerful. It can stir people to action, move them to tears of both joy and sorrow, and—as it did here—inflict great pain. On the facts before us, we cannot react to that pain by punishing the speaker. As a Nation we have chosen a different course—to protect even hurtful speech on public issues to ensure that we do not stifle public debate.[22]

In the only dissent, Justice Samuel Alito wrote,

Our profound national commitment to free and open debate is not a license for the vicious verbal assault that occurred in this case. Petitioner Albert Snyder is not a public figure. He is simply a parent whose son, Marine Lance Corporal Matthew Snyder, was killed in Iraq. Mr. Snyder wanted what is surely the right of any parent who experiences such an incalculable loss: to bury his son in peace. But respondents, members of the Westboro Baptist Church, deprived him of that elementary right.

Finally Justice Alito noted that WBC's "outrageous conduct caused petitioner great injury, and the Court now compounds that injury by depriving petitioner of a judgment that acknowledges the wrong he suffered. In order to have a society in which public issues can be openly and vigorously debated, it is not necessary to allow the brutalization of innocent victims like [the] petitioner. I therefore respectfully dissent."[23]

In August 2012, President Barack Obama signed legislation that counters the earlier Supreme Court decision. The new law Honoring America's Veterans and Caring for Camp Lejeune Families Act of 2012 covers a wide range of military benefits and restrictions. The restrictions affect groups like the WBC. "Under the new legislation, protests must be held at least 300 feet from military funerals and are prohibited two hours before or after a service," the *Huffington Post*'s Nick Wing reported.[24]

In recent years, students and faculty at numerous universities have called for censorship of hate speech and symbolism. All Western democracies have laws prohibiting hate speech, but the United States is the exception. As groups and individuals try to eradicate hate, they sometimes call for silencing repugnant speech, which may include not only verbal messages but also those on blogs, websites, signs, posters, pamphlets, and so forth. But, says the Florida chapter of the ACLU, "How much we value the right of free speech is put to its severest test when the speaker is someone we disagree with most. Speech that deeply offends our morality or is hostile to our way of life warrants the same constitutional

Even Liars Are Protected

Although much hate speech contains outright fabrications, lies of another variety are also protected speech. To promote themselves and their achievements, some people falsely claim to have won professional awards or earned military honors or medals. That was the case with Xavier Alvarez of California. He was convicted in February 2012 under the federal Stolen Valor Act of lying about receiving the nation's highest award for valor, the Medal of Honor. But Alvarez's attorneys argued that his false statements were protected by the First Amendment and on June 28, 2012, the U.S. Supreme Court agreed. The justices found the Stolen Valor Act unconstitutional and struck it down. However, the decision left open the possibility that the law could be rewritten so that it is constitutional. In September 2012, the U.S. House of Representatives passed a new Stolen Valor Act that makes it a crime to lie about a military record in order to obtain payment or other benefits. And in December 2012, the U.S. Senate passed an amendment to a defense authorization bill that is similar to the House's new act. A House bill introduced in January 2013 changed the act's previous language so it can withstand constitutional scrutiny.

protection as other speech because the right of free speech is indivisible: When one of us is denied this right, all of us are denied." Hate symbols also may be protected under the First Amendment "if they're displayed before a general audience in a public place, say, in a march or at a rally in a public park. But the First Amendment doesn't protect the use of nonverbal symbols to encroach upon, or desecrate, private property, such as burning a cross on someone's lawn or spray painting a swastika on the wall of a synagogue or dorm."[25]

Banning Religious Symbols and Attire in Public Schools—a Form of Bigotry?

When religious symbols and attire are banned in public schools, some people say the ban is an act of bigotry, especially as more and more students of diverse religious backgrounds attend public schools in the United States. For example, an orthodox or baptized male Sikh must wear a small, curved sword known as a *kirpan*, which symbolizes his religious duty to protect the weak and promote justice. Federal laws prohibit bringing weapons of any kind on school grounds, which has created a quandary for Sikh students. Some school districts have banned Sikh students from wearing the *kirpan* because the ceremonial item has been seen as a weapon.

In other types of bans, Muslim girls who wear the hijab, a religious head covering, have been told that the scarf violates school dress codes. Or school officials argue that federal law bans schools from encouraging any one religion over another. So a person might then ask, why not ban T-shirts with Christian messages such as "Jesus is my homeboy" or a Catholic student wearing ashes on his or her forehead on Ash Wednesday?

And what about religious symbols that students wear such as a Christian cross or a rosary? Some schools ban those symbols because gang members have adopted them to identify themselves. Jewish students also have been suspended (or threatened with suspension) for wearing a Star of David necklace because supposedly it looks like a gang symbol. Wiccan and pagan pentacles or pentagrams (five-pointed star in a circle) have been banned in schools because some officials say that Christians believe they are signs of the devil.

Whatever religious symbol a student may decide to wear, the symbol may stir a controversy or an attack by a classmate, as happened with Hadeiyah Ameen in 2010. As she explained, "During gym class, this one girl came up behind me and she pulled off my hijab. And my friend gives me this look and she walks up to the girl and she's like, 'If you ever touch her scarf again . . . ' All my other friends were really mad. They were like, 'We're never gonna talk to her again.'"[26]

Those who oppose students wearing religious symbols argue that "public schools are not saying that students cannot believe and practice their faith, just that they may not wear the symbols of their religions while on school grounds. They also state that public schools are religious-free zones; students go to school to learn, not to express their religious beliefs," writes a senior high school student who is a pagan and calls herself Ash. She adds, "Forbidding students to openly wear symbols of their religions at school is most definitely a violation of their rights and freedoms. The First Amendment states that. According to the United States Supreme Court, students' rights do not stop at the school door."[27]

Eighteen-year-old Aaron Zelikovich has often worn a yarmulke, or skullcap, because "it's meant to remind us that God is always above us, as well as he's always watching us," he explained. "So therefore we are more inclined to behave properly and do the right things, as we are instructed to do in the Bible." He added that the yarmulke "creates a sense of pride, like I'm Jewish and this is how I show that I'm Jewish, and that's for the whole world to see."[28]

In an article for *Y-Press*, three teenage Muslim students in Indianapolis, Indiana, told reporters why they wear the hijab: Amal Omar, age eighteen, said, "To me, it's more of a reminder of how I live my life. It's kind of a constant reminder throughout the day that I'm Muslim and I have certain ways that I act and how I represent Islam." Seventeen-year-old Nadiya Tai of India noted, "I recently started wearing a hijab, and it actually makes me feel very proud of my religion because instead of me being called a Hispanic or a Catholic or a Hindu, I am called a Muslim because of my scarf." When asked about reactions of people who fear Muslims and Islam, eighteen-year-old Hadeiyah Ameen said, "I can understand why some people are afraid because when you look at how the media portrays Muslims and Islam, from the first view you would get nervous and afraid. But once I smile at them, they kind of get this real relaxed feeling like, 'Oh, she's like any other person, she just looks a little different.' Just a scarf. Just a hijab, you know.'"[29]

So there is still a question: Should students be allowed to wear religious symbols and attire in public schools? If they are banned, is that a form of bigotry? What do you think?

Notes

1. Kari S., "Addressing Racism by Ignoring It," *Teen Ink*, n.d., www.teenink.com/opinion/discrimination/article/27028/Addressing-Racism-by-Ignoring-It (accessed June 10, 2012).
2. Rishi A., "English: The Official National Language," *Teen Ink*, n.d., www.teenink.com/opinion/all/article/10447/English-The-Official-National-Language/ (accessed April 20, 2012).
3. Asian Pacific American Legal Center of Southern California, "FACT SHEET: Why English Only–Legislation Violates the U.S. Constitution," n.d., www.advancingequality.org/files/fact_sheet_english_only_legislation.pdf (accessed April 18, 2012).

4. ACLU of Florida, "Take Action," n.d., www.aclufl.org/take_action/download_resources/info_papers/6.cfm (accessed April 18, 2012).

5. Lynnette Curtis, "Pahrump Targets Illegal Immigrants," *Las Vegas Review-Journal*, November 15, 2006, www.reviewjournal.com/lvrj_home/2006/Nov-15-Wed-2006/news/10847735.html (accessed June 9, 2012).

6. Ashley Powers, "As It Diversifies, Nevada Shifts Its Tone," *Los Angeles Times*, August 7, 2011, articles.latimes.com/print/2011/aug/07/nation/la-na-nevada-latinos-20110807 (accessed June 9, 2012).

7. Mark Waite, "Ethics Charges Upheld against Assessor, Fined $5,000," *Pahrump Valley Times*, April 20, 2012, pvtimes.com/news/ethics-charges-upheld-against-assessor-fined-5000/ (accessed June 9, 2012).

8. Jack Shakely, "Indian Mascots—You're Out," *Los Angeles Times*, August 25, 2011, articles.latimes.com/print/2011/aug/25/opinion/la-oe-shakely-teams-20110825 (accessed April 15, 2012).

9. Anti-Defamation League, "Hate on Display: A Visual Database of Extremist Symbols, Logos and Tattoos," n.d., www.adl.org/hate_symbols/default.asp (accessed April 23, 2012).

10. Staff of the Klanwatch Project, *Ku Klux Klan: A History of Racism and Violence*, 6th ed. (Montgomery, AL: Southern Poverty Law Center, 2011), 9, www.splcenter.org/sites/default/files/downloads/publication/Ku-Klux-Klan-A-History-of-Racism.pdf (accessed April 25, 2012).

11. Tom McNiff, "Patrons Mistake Ice Cream Shop Mascot for KKK Robes," *Ocala.com*, September 26, 2011, www.ocala.com/article/20110926/ARTICLES/110929750?template=print picart (accessed April 27, 2012).

12. Anti-Defamation League, "The National Socialist Movement," 2012, www.adl.org/Learn/Ext_US/nsm/default.asp?LEARN_Cat=Extremism&LEARN_SubCat=Extremism_in_America&xpicked=3&item=nsm (accessed April 28, 2012).

13. National Socialist Movement, "25 Points of American National Socialism," n.d., www.nsm88.org/25points/25pointsengl.html (accessed April 28, 2012).

14. Reclaim the Swastika, "History of the Swastika," n.d., reclaimtheswastika.com/history/ (accessed April 28, 2012).

15. 45th Infantry Division, "From Swastika to Thunderbird," n.d., www.45thdivisionmuseum.com/History/SwastikaToThunderbird.html (accessed April 28, 2012).

16. Mark Potok, "The Year in Hate and Extremism," *Intelligence Report*, Spring 2012, 40.

17. Joe Heim, "Wade Michael Page Was Steeped in Neo-Nazi 'Hate Music' Movement," *Washington Post*, August 7, 2012, www.washingtonpost.com/lifestyle/style/wade-michael-page-was-steeped-in-neo-nazi-hate-music-movement/2012/08/07/b879451e-dfe8-11e1-a19c-fcfa365396c8_print.html (accessed September 1, 2012).

18. Mark Pitcavage, "Op-Ed: Shine a Light on Hateful White Power Music," *JTA*, August 12, 2012, www.jta.org/news/article/2012/08/12/3103606/white-power-musics-powerful-anti-semitism (accessed September 1, 2012).

19. Patrick Condon and Todd Richmond, "Hate Music Is Part of White Supremacist Circles," *MPR News*, August 8, 2012, minnesota.publicradio.org/display/web/2012/08/08/crime/hate-music/ (accessed September 1, 2012).

20. United States Courts, "What Does Free Speech Mean?" United States Courts, n.d., www.uscourts.gov/EducationalResources/ClassroomActivities/FirstAmendment/WhatDoesFreeSpeechMean.aspx (accessed August 27, 2012).

21. Geoffrey Stone, "Remembering the Nazis in Skokie," *Huffington Post*, April 19, 2009, www .huffingtonpost.com/geoffrey-r-stone/remembering-the-nazis-in_b_188739.html (accessed June 18, 2012).

22. *Snyder v. Phelps et al.*, October 6, 2010, www.supremecourt.gov/opinions/10pdf/09-751.pdf (accessed April 30, 2012).

23. *Snyder v. Phelps et al.*

24. Nick Wing, "Honoring America's Veterans Act Signed by Obama, Restricting Westboro Military Funeral Protests," *Huffington Post*, August 6, 2012, www.huffingtonpost.com/ 2012/08/06/honoring-americas-veterans-act-obama_n_1748454.html (accessed August 27, 2012).

25. ACLU of Florida, "Hate Speech on Campus," 2012, www.aclufl.org/take_action/download_ resources/info_papers/16.cfm?print=true (accessed June 12, 2012).

26. Meera Patel and Daniel Ballow, "Religious Symbols," *Y-Press*, July 3, 2010, www.ypress.org/ news/religious_symbols (accessed June 9, 2012).

27. Ash, "The Ban on Religious Symbols in Public Schools," Darkness Embraced, last modi- fied August 5, 2011, www.darknessembraced.com/pagan-and-occult/pagan-and-neo-pagan -paths/item/204-the-ban-on-religious-symbols-in-public-schools (accessed May 2, 2012).

28. Patel and Ballow, "Religious Symbols."

29. Patel and Ballow, "Religious Symbols."

CENSORSHIP: AN ACT OF INTOLERANCE?

"You say Harry Potter books promote Satanism. It doesn't. Read the book. It is actually going against Satanism."—Fourteen-year-old Laura in a protest e-mail to a Georgia group using misleading statements to try to censor J. K. Rowling's books[1]

When people are intolerant or have bigoted opinions of other's views, they frequently attempt to censor expression of those views by, for example, preventing free speech, by blocking publication of articles and books, or by banning books in schools and libraries. "Should people be able to deny a student's freedom to read any book they wish to in a school?" asks Adam Weiner in a 2005 essay for an honors high school English class. "Every time adults ban a book, kids lose the chance to gain knowledge from that work of literature. The students' outlook on the world becomes narrower as they lose access to an insightful point of view. Book censors can only give unreasonable and unjustifiable motives for banning books to validate their cause. In the end, the actions of the people who ban books create many negative effects on students."[2]

However, those who want to censor what students read do not believe they are creating "negative effects on students." Neither do they think they are being intolerant or bigoted. Quite the opposite. In some cases, books are challenged or banned because they contain language that parents or librarians label as unsuitable, problematic, or offensive to young readers. Books with racial slurs and stories about sexual topics often are banned. "Many parents believe a book's subject matter condones a particular behavior or attitude; therefore they react negatively to books they perceive as offensive. When confronted, many schools react by pulling the books off the shelves themselves to avoid controversy. One school system headed off controversies by putting bright pink slips in controversial books to warn parents to examine the book before the child reads it," writes Kimberly Hartfield for *Knowledge Network*.[3]

Books about children with same-sex parents have been banned in numerous communities, and some politicians have submitted bills to prohibit the use of public funds to purchase textbooks or library materials that recognize homosexuality as an acceptable lifestyle. In some instances, parents, politicians, and religious groups challenge other books that they think are inappropriate for schools and public libraries to have on their shelves.

The American Library Association (ALA) says,

A challenge is an attempt to remove or restrict materials, based upon the objections of a person or group. A banning is the removal of those materials. Challenges do not simply involve a person expressing a point of view; rather, they are an attempt to remove material from the curriculum or library, thereby restricting the access of others. Due to the commitment of librarians, teachers, parents, students and other concerned citizens, most challenges are unsuccessful and most materials are retained in the school curriculum or library collection.[4]

One unsuccessful challenge took place in San Luis Obispo, California. A group of parents objected to *Kaffir Boy*, a memoir by Mark Mathabane, and wanted it censored by removing it from the high school shelves. The book is about growing up in South Africa when blacks and whites were strictly separated. Mathabane's autobiographical account was challenged by parents who objected to a description of boys prostituting themselves in order to obtain food. The parent group could not tolerate the sodomy scene and wanted it eliminated in an abridged version. However, when Mathabane was asked if he would allow an abridged version, his answer was simply no. Student Derek Chesnut, a high school junior noted, "We're old enough to read books like *Kaffir Boy*. I think it's offensive for parents to think it's their responsibility to parent other kids and not their own. . . . You're promoting ignorance."[5] The book remained in the school library.

It's a Fact

"The term censorship derives from the official duties of the Roman censor who, beginning in 443 B.C., conducted the census by counting, assessing, and evaluating the populace. Originally neutral in tone, the term has come to mean the suppression of ideas or images by the government or others with authority." So says *Encyclopedia.com*.[6]

Historical Practice

Over the centuries, some books have been banned because they contain scenes, language, and views considered objectionable by standards of the time. Although some people find book banning an act of censorship and intolerance, others believe censoring published materials protects social morality or the established political system.

In the past, books that have been banned or challenged have won Newbery, National Book, Pulitzer, or even Nobel prizes. For example, during the nineteenth century, books and other published material that contained information about birth control and sex education were considered obscene by the 1873 Comstock Act, named for Anthony Comstock, a special agent for the U.S. Post Office Department. Comstock was a zealous Christian who tried to impose his beliefs on the nation. He considered himself the moral guardian of the U.S. mail and became a powerful censor, crusading against birth-control advocates. He successfully lobbied for passage of the federal law that banned "lewd, obscene, and/or lascivious" books and other published materials from being sent through the mail.

Because of the Comstock Act, numerous people became victims of bigotry and intolerance. One was Ezra Heywood (1829–1893), an anarchist, abolitionist, and free-love, women's rights, and birth control advocate in Massachusetts. He was arrested in 1877 for publishing an essay titled *Cupid's Yokes*. He was convicted of sending obscene literature through the mail and in 1878 was sentenced to two years in prison. President Rutherford B. Hayes pardoned Heywood after he served six months. However, Heywood "was arrested four more times; three times he went free. On the fourth occasion, a conservative judge sent him back to prison for two years of hard labor. . . . He contracted tuberculosis in jail and died within a year of his release," according to the Mass Moments website.[7]

Another victim of intolerance was Margaret Sanger (1879–1966), who was indicted for advocating birth control in her 1914 publication *Woman's Rebel*. She fled to England and distributed a pamphlet titled *Family Liberation*, which contained information on sex, abortion, and birth control, including types of contraceptive methods. She returned to the United States to stand trial in 1915, but all charges against her were dropped. However, her ex-husband was jailed for thirty days for distributing Sanger's pamphlet.

Bigots attacked Mary Ware Dennett (1872–1947) when she wrote an essay for her sons—one a teenager and the other a preteen—who had been asking her questions about sex. She titled her essay "The Sex Side of Life: An Explanation for Young People," and used scientific terminology for the sex organs and illustrated it with her own drawings. She sent a copy of it to her sons and also loaned a copy of the essay to friends for their children. Later she published it as a pamphlet that was widely distributed by a variety of groups championing women's health and women's rights. In 1928, a woman complained to a U.S. Post Office inspector that her daughter had received a copy of Dennett's pamphlet in the mail. The inspector ordered a copy for himself, and after reading it began legal proceedings against Dennett. After many postponements, her trial began in 1929 and ended with a conviction on obscenity charges. But she appealed and her conviction was overturned. In his opinion, Circuit Court Judge Augustus Hand wrote, "We hold that an accurate exposition of the relevant facts of the sex side of life in decent language and in manifestly serious and disinterested spirit cannot ordinarily be regarded as obscene."[8]

Other published works that were banned because of the Comstock Law include Aristophanes' *Lysistrata*, a comedy about a woman who sets out to end the Peloponnesian War. In this ancient Greek play, Lysistrata brings Greek women together and convinces them to refuse to have sex with their husbands and lovers until the men negotiate peace. *Canterbury Tales* by the great fifteenth-century poet Geoffrey Chaucer, called the father of English literature, was banned because of sexual content and profanity. The Comstock Act in modified form still remains on the books. Restrictions on mailing contraceptive information are gone, but materials related to abortion are a violation of the Act and a 1996 amendment bans abortion-related materials on the Internet.

A Surge in Banned Books

During the 1980s, an increasing number of individuals and groups expressed their intolerance for various books in school libraries, which led to demands to censor or ban these books in schools. But those demands were resisted by parents, school personnel, and students who filed lawsuits to prevent book bans. "At that time, no legal precedents were in place to guide school administrators on appro-

Did You Know?

The *American Heritage Dictionary* published in 1969 has been banned several times. For example, "In 1978, an Eldon, Missouri, library banned the dictionary because it contained 39 'objectionable' words. And, in 1987, the Anchorage School Board banned the dictionary for similar reasons, that is, having slang definitions for words such as 'bed,' 'knocker,' and 'balls,'" according to the website wiki.ncac.org/American_Heritage_Dictionary.

priate responses to book challenges," report Amy Pelman and Beverly Lynch in the *Journal of Research on Libraries and Young Adults.* "As a result, in 1982, *Board of Education v. Pico* . . . reached the Supreme Court."[9]

The *Pico* case began years before, when New York's Island Trees High School student seventeen-year-old Steven Pico stood up for his First Amendment right to read books of his choice. In 1976, four school board members, in spite of objections by the school superintendent, removed nine books from the high school library and two books from the junior high library. Why? Because a conservative parent organization in Upstate New York had created a list of books that they labeled unfit for school libraries.

Board members did not specify why the books were "unfit" except to call them vulgar, anti-Christian, or anti-Semitic. The books removed included *Slaughterhouse-Five* by Kurt Vonnegut; *The Naked Ape* by Desmond Morris; *Down These Mean Streets* by Piri Thomas; *Best Short Stories by Negro Writers* by Langston Hughes; *Go Ask Alice* by Anonymous; *Laughing Boy* by Oliver La Farge; *Black Boy* by Richard Wright; *A Hero Ain't Nothin' but a Sandwich* by Alice Childress; and *Soul on Ice* by Eldridge Cleaver.

After the board's action the school superintendent "decided to call a meeting of Island Tree parents and citizens," according to Robert D. Morrow, professor emeritus of Pacific University, adding, "More than 500 attended. Many were furious at the board's action, demanding the books be returned to the library." Morrow reported that the superintendent declared, "'It is wrong to judge any book on the basis of brief excerpts provided by an Upstate New York group. It is wrong to take action based on a list prepared by someone outside the Island Trees Community. It is wrong to bypass the established procedure for reviewing the challenged books.' From there, the story became national news. Media poured into the tiny Long Island School District."[10] And Steven Pico along with some of his peers filed a lawsuit against the school board in the federal district court, which ruled in favor of the school board. However, in 1980 the U.S. Court of Appeals reversed the district court judgment. By 1982, the case—the first school library book banning case—was before the U.S. Supreme Court, which decided five to four in favor of Steven Pico and the other respondents.

In 1982, the ALA began its annual Banned Books Week to celebrate "the freedom to read and the importance of the First Amendment." In 2011, ALA celebrated its thirtieth Banned Books Week and listed the banned or challenged books in 2010–2011, which can be accessed at www.ala.org/advocacy/sites/ala.org.advocacy/files/content/banned/bannedbooksweek/ideasandresources/free_downloads/2011banned.pdf. The website also describes who challenged or banned the books and the reasons why. The ALA's annual Banned Books Week in 2012 was observed September 30–October 6 with the theme "30 Years of Liberating Literature."

Off the Bookshelf: Read a Banned Book

If you want to make up your own mind about whether a book should be banned, you can select one from those that have been challenged or actually pulled from bookshelves. Here are some examples:

- *The Absolutely True Diary of a Part-Time Indian* by Sherman Alexie, which won the National Book Award in 2007, is a semiautobiographical story of Arnold Spirit, a teenager on the Spokane Indian Reservation in Washington State. He is a cartoonist who enhances his chronicle with his drawings.
- *Anne Frank: The Diary of a Young Girl* by Anne Frank is a book about Nazi atrocities during World War II.
- *The Hunger Games* by Suzanne Collins was named Best Book of the Year in 2008 by *Publishers Weekly* and is the basis for a movie by the same title. The teenage heroine Katniss (Kat) lives in a futurist time in a nation called Panem, and is involved in a kill-or-be-killed game in an annual televised event called the Hunger Games.
- *Snow Falling on Cedars* by David Guterson is a book about discrimination against Japanese Americans during World War II.
- *The Notebook Girls: Four Friends, One Diary, Real Life* is by Julia Baskin, Lindsey Newman, Sophie Pollitt-Cohen, and Courtney Toombs. They describe their work as a book that "allowed us to express ourselves and our views of the world in a tone of complete sarcasm, obscenity, and blind honesty."
- *The Adventures of Huckleberry Finn* by Mark Twain is a book that has been banned repeatedly because of the pejorative word *nigger*, which was commonly used in the mid-nineteenth century at the time and place of the book's setting.
- *Of Mice and Men* by John Steinbeck—a story of two migrant workers—has been banned or challenged repeatedly because of profanity.

Nevertheless, books continue to be removed from school shelves. A case of book banning made news headlines in February 2012, when Arizona's superintendent of public instruction ordered the Tucson Unified School District to remove books about Mexican Americans from classrooms. The state had passed a new law banning ethnic studies, on the grounds that studying about ethnic or racial groups promoted hatred and division. Under the law, books about Mexico and Mexican Americans were considered ethnic studies and banned. Superintendent John Huppenthal informed the school district that the books had to be pulled from the shelves. If the district did not comply it would lose millions of dollars in state funds. Books were taken from the schools and locked away in a warehouse.

The Arizona ban on ethnic studies and books sparked dissent in various parts of the nation. In St. Paul, Minnesota, Central High School students and teachers protested on February 16, 2012. One student, Deja Whitfield, told a reporter, "It's kind of ironic to ban books from Latinos because of controversial stuff in poems and plays, when white people in Arizona are actually doing controversial stuff. . . . We need information to make this stop." Ekeylie Lee, another student, said, "It's wrong for one ethnicity to have the upper hand, wrong for one to be able to express themselves and the others not be able to." Student Shevell Powell

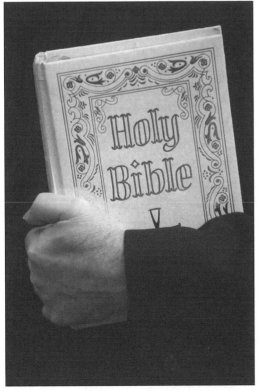 

The Bible and the Quran (also spelled Koran) are two books that have been burned in protests.

put it this way: "We need to learn about every culture. . . . We should not ban Latino culture. We need to learn more about it."[11]

Burning Books

When a discussion about burning books comes up, comments often center on the Nazis in Germany in 1933 when dictator Adolf Hitler and the German Student Association gathered books considered un-German. Students burned more than twenty-five thousand books in a public display of intolerance, bigotry, and hatred.

Yet, book burning has taken place in centuries past at least since 213 B.C. when books by Confucius and other works were burned by the Qin dynasty in China in an attempt to wipe out China's history. "Perhaps the most famous burning of all time occurred at the Royal Library at Alexandria, Egypt, one of the great repositories of learning in the ancient world, which held 40,000 manuscripts, many irreplaceable," writes David Serchuk in *Forbes* magazine. "Accounts differ about who ultimately burned the library; some say it was Julius Caesar in 47 or 48 B.C., who torched it inadvertently during battle with his arch-enemy Pompey. Others say the decisive burning occurred in 642 A.D., upon the orders of Omar, the Second Caliph of Islam."[12]

Books are torched for many reasons, such as moral, political, and religious beliefs. Usually, the books that get burned are considered heretical, blasphemous, subversive, obscene, or immoral by varied groups. In 1520, Martin Luther (1483–1546), a leader of the Protestant Reformation, burned Catholic books that asserted the authority of the pope. The Bible "has been frequently burned," according to *Forbes* writer Serchuk. "William Tyndale is perhaps little remembered today, but in 1526, he printed the first-ever New Testament in English. The Bishop of London, not happy to see the Word so easily put in the hands of the laity, hunted Tyndale and his books down, burning them."[13]

In the United States, intolerance and bigotry have led to censoring books by burning them. The first perhaps was in 1650, when a public executioner burned the religious book *A Meritorious Price of Our Redemption* by William Pynchon (1590–1662), one of the founders of the Massachusetts Bay Colony. A court determined that the publication was heretical.

In the 1700s, German immigrant John Peter Zenger (1697–1746), a printer and publisher of the *New York Weekly Journal*, was arrested and charged with printing editions of the newspaper that allegedly contained seditious libel against the corrupt New York governor. To censor Zenger, the city council exhibited their intolerance by recommending that various editions be burned. Zenger went to trial and admitted he had printed copies of the *Journal*. Although the judge instructed the jury to find Zenger guilty, the jury exonerated him because he had printed the truth, which is not libel.

In the late 1940s, various groups—including the National Parent-Teachers Association, the U.S. Conference of Mayors, and officials in some U.S. cities— were intolerant of comic books, which they deemed immoral and feared would corrupt youth. Comic books were gathered in cities from Sacramento, California, to Coral Gables, Florida. Students often took part to demonstrate their "moral" behavior and burned the comics in public displays.

In the 1950s, Wisconsin senator Joseph McCarthy was blatantly intolerant of anyone he thought was a communist or communist sympathizer. He falsely accused many Americans, including members of the U.S. Army, of being communists, destroying the careers of hundreds. In another demonstration of his intolerance and bigotry, McCarthy also gathered and burned hundreds of books written by authors he labeled communists.

In the twenty-first century, book burnings still occur because of intolerance and bigotry. The Harry Potter series by J. K. Rowling prompted the Christ Community Church in Alamogordo, New Mexico, to set a bonfire in 2001 to destroy Harry Potter books, which the pastor called "a masterpiece of satanic deception." Accusing the books of promoting Satanism is common among some fundamentalist Christian churches.

When fourteen-year-old Laura of Georgia read about a church group attacking *Harry Potter*, she sent a protest e-mail that said in part: "You turn around what readers and the books say. I bet that you are going to twist what I am saying right now, and say that I am for Satanism. Well, I am not. You don't give complete quotes, and you don't say if it is an evil character saying the words or not. If you don't give the whole truth, you are telling a lie. And from what your webpage tells me, you are Christian, and isn't telling a lie against one of the ten commandments. YES!!!! It clearly states: 'Thou shall not give false testimony against your neighbor.'"[14]

A rural Pennsylvania Harvest Assembly of God Church burned Rawlings's books in 2001. In Lewiston, Maine, a group planned to burn Harry Potter books, but the town would not issue a permit. So in a 2001 public ceremony the group shredded the books instead. The group held a similar ceremony in 2002. The Jesus Non-Denominational Church in Michigan set fire to Harry Potter books in 2003, which led intolerant and bigoted spectators to add other books to the flames: the Book of Mormon and a non–King James version of the Bible.

Sometimes fundamentalist Christians use a biblical verse to justify book burning. Acts 19:19–20 (in the revised standard edition) describes those who repented after being involved in occult practices. The verses state, "And a number of those who practiced magic arts brought their books together and began burning them in the sight of all; and they counted up the price of them and found it came to fifty thousand pieces of silver. So the word of the Lord grew and prevailed mightily." It is unclear from the verses what the price of the burned books had to do with "the word of the Lord" prevailing.

Since the terrorist attacks on U.S. soil in 2001, in acts of religious bigotry, the Quran (Koran), the Muslim holy book, has been singled out for burning. In 2010, Terry Jones, a pastor of a small evangelical church called the Dove World Outreach Center in Gainesville, Florida, publicly announced that he would burn copies of the Quran to protest the building of an Islamic center near the site of the World Trade Center in New York City destroyed by terrorists. Government officials and religious leaders persuaded him to give up the protest, arguing that the book burning would incite a violent response. Jones promised not to conduct the burning. However, in March 2011, Jones burned a copy of the Quran, which was placed in a metal tray in the center of the church and torched with a barbecue lighter. But the Quran-burning pastor was not finished with his protests. In June 2012, he hung an effigy of President Obama outside his church in Gainesville, Florida. Andres Jauregui noted in the *Huffington Post*, "The effigy is suspended from a makeshift gallows with a noose of yellow rope, has a doll in its right hand and a rainbow-colored gay pride flag in its left. . . . Jones said the flag was meant to call attention to Obama's stance on same-sex marriage and that the baby doll is there because the president is 'favorable toward abortion.'"[15]

In 2012, U.S. service members burned Qurans at Bagram Air Field, the largest North Atlantic Treaty Organization base in Afghanistan. According to military officials and President Obama, the act was unintentional. "U.S. service members were following orders to burn the Korans and other reading materials that may or may not have been used by Afghan inmates to pass encoded messages between themselves at Parwan Detention Facility, which adjoins the base. . . . The burning took place in view of local Afghan staff who felt compelled to get word of the action out to the population at large," writes Allison Stanger, professor of international politics and economics and chair of the Political Science Department at Middlebury College in Vermont. President Obama apologized for the burning, but protests erupted in Afghanistan and U.S. soldiers were killed. Obama was criticized in the United States for apologizing, but as Stanger notes, "We should never implicitly condone American soldiers burning books as a means to defending freedom by attacking those who apologize. The cost of losing what we are fighting to uphold is far too high."[16]

Censoring by Revising

While banning books from school and public library shelves and burning books are forms of intolerance and censorship, other types of censorship go on. That has been the case for *The Adventures of Huckleberry Finn*, a novel that has been censored by revision as well as by removal from school shelves. One version published in 2011 by New South Books replaces the word *nigger* (used more than two hundred times) with *slave* and the word *injun* with *Indian*. These changes were devised by Alan Gribben, an English professor in Alabama, who was concerned that the racial slurs in the book offended many readers. But the revisions upset many English teachers, librarians, and others who believe Mark Twain's work should be left alone. As one writer Michiko Kakutani points out in the *New York Times*, "attaching the epithet slave to the character Jim—who has run away in a bid for freedom—effectively labels him as property, as the very thing he is trying to escape." When a work is revised, Kakutani writes,

> it relieves teachers of the fundamental responsibility of putting such books in context—of helping students understand that *Huckleberry Finn* actually stands as a powerful indictment of slavery (with Nigger Jim its most noble character), of using its contested language as an opportunity to explore the painful complexities of race relations in this country. To censor or redact books on school reading lists is a form of denial: shutting the door on harsh historical realities—whitewashing them or pretending they do not exist.[17]

Some censors have actually blacked out various words in a book, such as Ray Bradbury's *Fahrenheit 451*. One high school version of the book deleted such words as *Jesus Christ*, *hell*, and *dammit*, but as soon as Bradbury heard about it he contacted his publisher. Within a few days that excised version was gone.

In some cases, censorship of books and other published materials for schools occurs silently—in the minds of teachers, librarians, publishers, and others who choose what students will read. It's called silent censorship. The process of self-censorship for textbooks may begin with publishers who comply with demands from a variety of groups who have no tolerance for teaching evolution, so such information does not appear in texts. Or publishers may be pressured to eliminate any mention of multiracial families or same-sex couples or dead animals or extreme violence or just about any other matter that someone or some group finds objectionable. Teachers and librarians also take part in silent censorship by deciding not to buy or recommend a book because of specific words or controversial topics in a text. In other words, a type of bigotry prevails when only one view is allowed to exist—the censor's way is right and everyone else is wrong or misguided.

Censoring Websites in Schools

Access Denied are the boldfaced words that sometimes confront students who try to log on to some websites that their schools or public libraries have blocked with filtering software. Some librarians, teachers, and students argue that blocking websites is an intolerant practice. Yet the Children's Internet Protection Act of 2000 requires schools and libraries to use filtering software if they receive federal funding for Internet access on their computers. That is, filter software must block Internet access to material that is obscene, pornographic, or harmful to minors. The law has been challenged as violating First Amendment rights and thus as unconstitutional, but the U.S. Supreme Court upheld the act even though the justices acknowledged that a filter could block sites that are not objectionable and could be educational for minors.

One example is filtering sites about drug awareness because the keyword *drugs* results in a filter that blocks access. In other instances sites that contain information about lesbian, gay, bisexual, and transgender (LGBT) issues and organizations may be blocked. That situation occurred in 2009 when the American Civil Liberties Union (ACLU) filed a lawsuit against Metropolitan Nashville Public Schools and Knox County Schools (Tennessee) on behalf of three high school students in Nashville, one student in Knoxville, and a high school librarian in Knoxville. The schools were using filtering software that blocked access to websites about LGBT issues. "However, the filter did not block access to Web sites that urge LGBT persons to change their sexual orientation or gender identity through so-called 'reparative therapy' or 'ex-gay' ministries—a practice denounced as dangerous and harmful to young people by such groups as the American Psychological Association and the American Medical Association," noted an ACLU press release. The schools ended their censorship and the lawsuit was dropped. "Schools that censor educational information out of some misguided assumption that anything about LGBT people is automatically sexual or inappropriate are doing a disservice to their students," said ACLU's staff attorney.[18]

Censorship of websites may also occur when parents and educators are concerned that students will become victims of cyberbullying, which has led to tragic suicides. Another concern is students browsing Facebook, YouTube, Twitter, and similar sites when they should be paying attention in class.

Justine Nason, a student at Ashland (Maine) District School, is against censoring social websites, stating in the high school's newspaper, "A website like Youtube can provide educational material. Some teachers in Ashland District School use Youtube for educational purposes. . . . users also post things such as how-to videos and plays their class preformed."[19]

The American Association of School Librarians (AASL) notes, "Filtering websites does the next generation of digital citizens a disservice. Students must develop skills to evaluate information from all types of sources in multiple formats, *including the Internet.* Relying solely on filters does not teach young citizens how to be savvy searchers or how to evaluate the accuracy of information." On September 28, 2011, the AASL established the first annual Banned Websites

It Happened to SOPA and PIPA

No. These aren't people. They are acronyms for two congressional bills introduced in 2011: the Stop Online Piracy Act (SOPA) that the U.S. House of Representatives was considering and Protect Internet Property Act (PIPA) a companion proposal in the U.S. Senate. The proposals were meant to prevent the piracy of copyrighted material such as music and films as well as manufactured goods like counterfeit watches. Among organizations supporting such legislation are the U.S. Chamber of Commerce and the Motion Picture Association of America.

If the bills had passed, they would have shut down some websites, including social media. For opponents of the bills, blocking social media would be an intolerant act and would suppress free speech. In a protest piece for the Ashland District School newspaper in Maine, high school student Justine Nason wrote, "Websites such as Youtube [sic] or Wikipedia, which people not only enjoy being on, can also be used as a learning tool. If an education video has a copyrighted song on it as background music, it can be taken down. If an interesting or informative article has something on it that is copyrighted, such as a certain link, it can be taken down."[20]

In another protest article, staff writer Christian Gin for the *Spartan Daily* at San Jose State University in California wrote, "Videos would have to have only original content everywhere. Whether it's music, video or pictures, it has to be someone's own material rather than a song by an artist or picture by a famous photographer. . . . The ability to put something on YouTube would be very limited to things someone filmed with their camera."[21]

These student arguments were not isolated. The technology industry joined in protesting the congressional bills. Wikipedia blacked out for one day, and Google placed a black marker over its logo and asked viewers to sign a petition against SOPA and PIPA. As *Forbes* magazine Larry Magid noted,

Silicon Valley has invested billions in creating companies that freely distribute information. While Google and every other Silicon Valley company must respect copyrights, they thrive on helping people find what they want. If, suddenly, every web site that had links to other sites had to worry that they could be in violation of the law by linking to a "banned" site, it could put undo [sic] pressure on these companies. There is also worry that SOPA and PIPA could be abused and lead to censorship for purposes other than intellectual property protection.[22]

By the end of January 2012, SOPA and PIPA were tabled. "Lawmakers abandoned the bills after tech companies and groups, along with ordinary Internet users, mounted a frenzy of protests, saying the bills would hurt Internet freedom and innovation," according to the *New York Times*.[23] Yet, the bills could appear again in modified form.

Awareness Day "as an offshoot of Banned Books Week to highlight the harmful effects of censorship in schools." The event has taken place every year since.[24]

Notes

1. Laura, "Kids Speak Out on Harry Potter!" KidSpeak, 2001, www.kidspeakonline.org/kids saying2.html (accessed June 9, 2012).
2. Adam Weiner, "Banning Books Is Bad for Students," BookRags, November 21, 2005, www .bookrags.com/essay-2005/11/30/191721/03 (accessed May 5, 2012).
3. Kimberly Hartfield, "Conflicts of Censorship Pros and Cons," Knoji, n.d., general-law.knoji .com/conflicts-of-censorship-the-pros-and-cons/ (accessed May 5, 2012).
4. American Library Association, "About Banned & Challenged Books," n.d., www.ala.org/ advocacy/banned/aboutbannedbooks (accessed May 5, 2012).
5. Patrick S. Pemberton, "'Kaffir Boy' Stirs Up Censorship Talk at San Luis Obispo High School," *Tribune* (San Luis Obispo, California), October 16, 2010, http://www.sanluisobispo .com/2010/10/16/1331758/kaffir-boy-stirs-up-censorship.html (December 12, 2012).
6. See www.encyclopedia.com/topic/censorship.aspx (accessed December 7, 2012).
7. Massachusetts Foundations for the Humanities, "August 1, 1787: Free Love Supporters Protest at Faneuil Hall," Mass Moments, August 1, 2005, www.massmoments.org/print_ moment.cfm?mid=223 (accessed May 14, 2012).
8. Constance W. Chen, *"The Sex Side of Life": Mary Ware Dennett's Pioneering Battle for Birth Control and Sex Education* (New York: The New Press, 1996), 301.
9. Amy Pelman and Beverly Lynch, posted by Stephanie Kuenn, "The School Library versus the School Board: An Exploration of the Book Banning Trend of the 1980s," *Journal of Research on Libraries and Young Adults*, February 14, 2011, www.yalsa.ala.org/jrlya/2011/02/ the-school-library-versus-the-school-board-an-exploration-of-the-book-banning-trend-of -the-1980s/ (accessed May 8, 2012).

10. Robert D. Morrow, "Two Heroes Who Stood Their Ground," Recordnet.com, May 6, 2012, www.recordnet.com/apps/pbcs.dll/article?AID=/20120506/A_OPINION08/205060307/-1/ NEWSMAP (accessed May 8, 2012).

11. Mary Turck, "Central High School Students, Teachers Read Banned Books, Protesting Arizona Censorship," *Twin Cities Daily Planet*, February 16, 2012, www.tcdailyplanet.net/ news/2329/10/22/st-paul-notes-central-high-school-students-teachers-read-banned-books -protesting-ari?print=1 (accessed May 16, 2012).

12. David Serchuk, "Harry Potter and the Ministry of Fire," *Forbes*, December 1, 2006, www .forbes.com/2006/11/30/book-burnings-potter-tech-media_cz_ds_books06_1201burn_ print.html (accessed May 12, 2012).

13. Serchuk, "Harry Potter and the Ministry of Fire."

14. Laura, "Kids Speak Out on Harry Potter!"

15. Andres Jauregui, "Terry Jones, Quran-Burning Pastor, Hangs Barack Obama Effigy outside Florida Church," *Huffington Post*, June 8, 2012, www.huffingtonpost.com/2012/06/08/obama -effigy-hanged-outside-church_n_1581272.html?ref=topbar (accessed June 10, 2012).

16. Allison Stanger, "Allison Stanger: The U.S. Should Never Be Burning Books," *CNN*, February 26, 2012, globalpublicsquare.blogs.cnn.com/2012/02/26/stanger-the-u-s-should-never -be-burning-books/ (accessed May 8, 2012).

17. Michiko Kakutani, "Light Out, Huck, They Still Want to Sivilize You," *New York Times*, January 6, 2011, www.nytimes.com/2011/01/07/books/07huck.html?pagewanted=all&_r=0 (accessed December 10, 2012).

18. American Civil Liberties Union, "Tennessee Schools and Students Reach Settlement in Internet Censorship Case" (press release), August 13, 2009, www.aclu.org/print/free-speech_lgbt -rights/tennessee-schools-and-students-reach-settlement-internet-censorship-case (accessed May 19, 2012).

19. Justine Nason, "No Internet Censoring," *my.hsj.org*, February 27, 2012, my.hsj.org/Schools/ Newspaper/tabid/100/view/frontpage/articleid/503970/newspaperid/3896/No_Internet_ Censoring.aspx (May 19, 2012).

20. Nason, "No Internet Censoring."

21. Christian Gin, "ACTA, SOPA and PIPA Would Destroy the Internet," *Spartan Daily*, January 24, 2012, spartandaily.com/62827/acta-sopa-and-pipa-would-destroy-the-internet (accessed May 20, 2012).

22. Larry Magid, "What Are SOPA and PIPA and Why All the Fuss?" *Forbes*, January 18, 2012, www.forbes.com/sites/larrymagid/2012/01/18/what-are-sopa-and-pipa-and-why-all-the -fuss/print/ (accessed May 20, 2012).

23. "Copyrights and Internet Piracy (SOPA and PIPA Legislation)," *New York Times*, updated February 8, 2012, topics.nytimes.com/top/reference/timestopics/subjects/c/copyrights/ index.html (accessed May 20, 2012).

24. American Association of School Librarians, "Banned Websites Awareness Day," n.d., www .ala.org/aasl/aaslissues/bwad/bwad (accessed May 19, 2012).

HOW HATE GROUPS PROMOTE BIGOTRY

"As a black student, those words [white pride] scared and concerned me. A lot of other students and I feel unsafe . . . being on campus."—Kenan Herbert, a senior and president of the Black Student Union at Towson University in Baltimore, explaining the effect of "white pride" chalked on campus sidewalks[1]

"Who hires a hate group to lead a school assembly?" That is the question Mary Elizabeth Williams asks in the title to her article in *Salon.com*.[2] She is referring to Bradlee Dean and his Junkyard Prophet band that performed at a Dunkerton, Iowa, high school assembly in March 2012. The band is part of the You Can Run, But You Cannot Hide ministry, which the Southern Poverty Law Center (SPLC) has designated an antigay hate group. SPLC monitors all types of hate groups and antigovernment militia.

After performing, Dean and others in his ministry were supposed to deliver messages on tolerance and against bullying and drug use. Instead, junior and senior high school students were divided by gender. Members of the ministry herded girls to one room and boys to another. Faculty were sent in a different direction. In a speech, Dean told girls they would have "mud on their wedding dresses" if they were not virgins when they married. "The presentations included images of aborted fetuses and AIDS patients suffering the effects of the disease, according to students. Those who tried to leave, including teachers, were shouted down, mocked and intimidated," the *Waterloo-Cedar Falls Courier* reported. Dean also lambasted homosexuality.

Senior student eighteen-year-old Laura Steffen told a reporter, "They were really trying to push their religion down our throats." Two other seniors, twins Brandi and Randi Smith, who say they are "very Christian," agreed with some of the ministry's message, but noted, "The whole school's like way tense. No one's getting along anymore," Brandi said. Randi added, "I don't think that kind of message should have been given in a school." Still, the girls did not blame the school for allowing the band members to hold the assembly. Rather they blamed the band for falsely representing themselves.[3]

Mary Elizabeth Williams reports in *Salon.com*, "It didn't take long for word of Dean's grotesque presentation to get around—helped by the fact that his organization proudly posted clips of it on YouTube. It's a jaw-dropping performance, one in which Dean tells students that 'Planned Parenthood gives you coupons to get abortions' and declares, 'The average age death of a homosexual male is 42 years old. Yeah, his actions literally kill him.'. . . For his part, Dean insists that his appearance at Dunkerton High was 'a legitimate and challenging presentation' and that he is '100 percent certain' God appreciated his efforts."[4] One has to wonder what kind of god appreciates such intolerance and bigotry.

Antihomosexual Hate Groups Increase

Along with the Bradlee Dean band, the SPLC has added ten other groups to the organization's list of designated antigay hate groups. These are United Families International, Save California, Sons of Thundr (Faith Baptist Church), Parents Action League, Jewish Political Action Committee, Mission: America, Windsor Hills Baptist Church, True Light Pentecost Church, Tom Brown Ministries, and Public Advocate of the United States. Who are these groups and what are they all about? Here are some brief explanations:

- United Families International of Gilbert, Arizona, has argued that no one is born homosexual. "Policies that would normalize homosexuality by equating homosexual behavior with innate characteristics such as race or ethnicity should be opposed."[5]
- Save California of Sacramento "is leading the effort to recall a law requiring schools to incorporate the contributions of gay and lesbian Americans into the history curriculum." Randy Thomasson, a member of this group, "is claiming that 'gay activists' are 'kidnapping the brains of kids' by encouraging them to learn about the existence of gay people."[6]
- Sons of Thundr (Faith Baptist Church) in Luthersville, Georgia, have a website that claims in caps: "ALL HOMOS ARE: SICK, BRAIN DAMAGED, PERVERTS!"[7]
- Parents Action League of Champlin, Minnesota, is a small group of parents in Anoka-Hennepin School District, where there has been extensive gay harassment and bullying. The parents object to any educational materials about homosexuals and want a special section of the school's website devoted to "students of faith, moral conviction, ex-homosexuals, and ex-transgenders," which would be unconstitutional under the First Amendment.

- Jewish Political Action Committee of Brooklyn, New York, an ultra-orthodox group, claims that marriage equality in New York State has created a "surge" of child molestation and distributes signs that say "G-d sent AIDS to punish male gays." In addition they call President Obama a "Black Dog" and an "Arab."[8]
- Mission: America in Columbus, Ohio, is headed by Linda Harvey, who declares that "there continues to be no evidence homosexuality is inborn or pre-determined. Despite the fervent wishes and claims of many advocates, science has not accepted any research as validating a biological origin. The assumption that this has been 'decided' is everywhere, but it's not true, and to embrace this idea is to violate Christian doctrine as well as science."[9]
- Windsor Hills Baptist Church of Oklahoma City, Oklahoma, is headed by Pastor Tom Vineyard. He argued against the city's employment nondiscrimination proposal by falsely claiming that half of all murders in large cities are by gay people.[10]
- True Light Pentecost Church (Spartanburg, South Carolina). On the church's blog, it warns, "The sub-human culture created by the anti-christ and magnified by the Sodomite/Lesbian movement," has "brought end-time prophecy to a final state," and encourages followers to "fight the great sodomite/lesbian army."[11]
- Tom Brown Ministries in El Paso, Texas, headed by Pastor Tom Brown, has been leading an effort to rescind a city law that prevents workplace discrimination against homosexuals because in his view it condones immoral behavior.

❓ Did You Know?

A *hate crime* is defined as violent intolerance and bigotry, intended to hurt and intimidate people because of their race, ethnicity, national origin, religion, sexual orientation, or disability. The purveyors of hate use explosives, arson, weapons, vandalism, physical violence, and verbal threats of violence to instill fear in their victims, leaving them vulnerable to more attacks and feeling alienated, helpless, suspicious, and fearful. The U.S. Federal Bureau of Investigation (FBI) notes that the term *hate crime* did not enter the nation's vocabulary until the 1980s, when emerging hate groups like the Skinheads launched a wave of bias-related crime. The FBI began investigating what are now called hate crimes as far back as World War I, when the Ku Klux Klan first attracted national attention.

- Public Advocate of the United States of Falls Church, Virginia, is headed by Loudoun County (Virginia) Supervisor Eugene Delguaido (a Republican). This group is infamous for its over-the-top antigay fundraising letters, including comments such as, "As homosexuals die off due to AIDS, the remaining AIDS carriers prey on children to replenish the 'Homosexual Community.'"[12]

When Hate and Racism Destroyed an Entire Town

It happened decades ago—in 1923 to be exact—but the destruction of Rosewood, Florida, still resonates in current times. In fact, students at Eastside High School in Gainesville, Florida, learned about Rosewood in February 2012 and were aghast at what they saw and heard in a presentation by Marvin Dunn, director of an archaeological investigation of the town. Students had no real experience with the kind of gruesome brutality that occurred in the period following World War I, although they were well aware of racism and talked about the Gainesville High School students who in February 2012 presented a racist rant on a video. That rant, noted seventeen-year-old Elizabeth Osmun, "is not just racism, it's ignorance."[13]

Dunn, of Florida International University, wants students to be educated about history because "the more information you have, the less vulnerable you are to ignorance."[14] He showed photographs of the bloated bodies of Rosewood black men who had been lynched, which caused students to gasp in horror. But that was just one part of the story known as the Rosewood Massacre.

Rosewood was a small, rural village in Levy County, Florida, populated primarily by African Americans. Like other black communities in the United States after World War I, Rosewood residents frequently were targets for violence. From 1917 to 1923, "white mobs pursued what can only be described as a reign of terror against African Americans" whether they lived in big cities across the United States or in small towns, according to a report about Rosewood submitted to the Florida Board of Regents.[15] In Florida, four black men in McClenny were taken from jail in August 1920 and lynched for allegedly raping a white woman. In February 1921, a black man in Wauchula, Florida, was accused of attacking a white woman and was lynched. In Perry, a black man was accused of murdering a white school teacher; he was burned at the stake in December 1922.

On January 1, 1923, Fannie Taylor, a white woman who was having an extramarital affair, was beaten by her lover but said an unidentified black man attacked her. That falsehood prompted a series of horrific events during the first week of January 1923. White vigilantes gathered and a mob lynched a black man named Sam Carter. On January 4, white vigilantes attacked the home of Sarah Carrier.

Her son Sylvester Carrier had brought his family to his mother's home where he thought he could better protect them from white mobs. A gun fight ensued and Sarah Carrier was killed by a shot into the house. Other black residents who were hiding outside opened fire and shot or injured some of the white mob. During a cease-fire, Rosewood residents escaped into the nearby swamp.

Following the attack on the Carriers, white mobs set the house on fire and two to three hundred whites torched the entire village, except for the home of white store owner John Wright, who had taken in and hidden black residents seeking refuge. No one was ever charged for the crimes, and for decades few historians wrote about the violence and destruction at Rosewood. Survivors did not talk publicly about what they had witnessed, fearing retaliation. Finally, the Florida Department of Law Enforcement investigated the case in 1993, which led to legislation in 1994 that compensated each survivor of the massacre with $100,000 or more.

Since the late 1990s, bus tours of the ghost town have been conducted from Gainesville. And Rosewood is memorialized by such presentations as those of Marvin Dunn and by websites such as Remembering Rosewood at www .displaysforschools.com/history.html, Africana Online at www.africanaonline .com/2010/08/the-rosewood-massacre/, and the report to the Florida Board of Regents at www.displaysforschools.com/rosewoodrp.html.

Hate Groups Increase Nationwide

In 2010 SPLC counted a total of 1,002 active hate groups in the United States. In 2011 the total number jumped to 1,018. Most of them are in California (84) and southern states such as Florida (55), Texas (45), Tennessee (39), and Alabama (33). New Jersey also has a large number—47. These groups preach antigovernment doctrines or racist/bigoted views through websites, publications, speeches, and political campaigns.

Hate groups have increased in number in part because of the election of President Barack Obama, according to a variety of news reports and organizations that track racist/hate activities. Frequently white power groups express their hatred of the president because of their unsubstantiated belief that Obama was not born in America, that the United States is being "invaded" by nonwhites, and that ethnic and racial diversity is destroying U.S. culture.

Added to the overt hatred are politicians and talk show hosts who make comments and jokes that provide support for racism, bigotry, and intolerance. Some public figures have referred to Obama with terms such as "tar baby" (a tar-covered doll used to lure B'rer Rabbit in the Uncle Remus stories of the slave era), "African witch doctor," "food stamp president" (suggesting falsely that only people of color receive food stamps), and "skinny ghetto crackhead," and have displayed cartoons that present Obama as a Hitler-like caricature, a chimpanzee, or some other disparaging image.

While it's not possible to describe all the hate groups here, groups of particular interest and concern include the well-known Ku Klux Klan (KKK; discussed in chapter 7), neo-Nazis, members of the Christian Identity movement, Sovereign Citizens, black separatists, and white nationalists. Often these groups are intertwined in their intolerance and their hate-filled beliefs.

Neo-Nazis

Most neo-Nazis worship Adolf Hitler, who led the National Socialist German Workers' Party, or Nazi Party, founded in 1919. Early in his life, Hitler developed a hatred of Jews and was obsessed with a false notion that Jews around the world were involved in a conspiracy to destroy what he called the Aryan race. Once Hitler gained control of Germany in 1933, he set out to conquer Eastern Europe and attempted to establish his so-called superior society that resulted in the horrendous Holocaust.

While the Nazi Party never gained large numbers of members in the United States, neo-Nazis became well entrenched during the 1980s. In 2011, there were 170 U.S. groups that still follow the Hitler doctrine, espouse white power and white supremacy, often wear military garb, and practice guerrilla maneuvers. They have headquarters in such cities as Daytona, Florida; Zion, Illinois; Detroit, Michigan; and Tulsa, Oklahoma. Like other hate groups, they are likely to support the white supremacy doctrines of Christian Identity, or simply Identity, that champion a virulent anti-Semitic and racist theology.

Christian Identity

Preaching pseudo-Christian teachings, the Identity movement has a "two-seed" theory of humankind's origins. Unlike the biblical story that Adam and Eve produced two sons, Cain and Abel, Identity followers say that instead the two sons were Abel and Seth. After the boys were born, according to the Identity movement, Eve had sexual intercourse with Satan and produced another son, Cain, who murdered Abel. Seth's offspring (descendants of Adam) supposedly make up the white race, or what are called the Lost Tribes of the House of Israel or the true Israelites. Cain's descendants—Jews and blacks—are considered not fully human and have no souls. It is the mission of Christian Identity movement to rid the world of people who are not true Israelites. Identity groups are known by such names as America's Promise Ministries, Church of Jesus Christ Christians/Aryan Nation, and Yaweh's Truth.

Sovereign Citizens

Linked to the Identity movement are members of Sovereign Citizens, which began as Posse Comitatus. The latter was a loosely organized antigovernment and anti-Semitic group of radicals who called people of color and Jews "mud races." *Posse Comitatus* is a Latin term for "power of the county" and is based on the belief that Americans should be armed and prepared for action against "enemies" in Washington, D.C. Henry L. Beach, a member of the Hitler-like Silver Shirts of the 1930s, initiated Posse Comitatus in Portland, Oregon, in 1969. Followers believed they had the right to organize local governments with the local sheriff as the top elected governmental figure. The sheriff, in their view, should not be controlled by state or federal laws, and Posse Comitatus followers do not have to abide by most laws or pay taxes. Posse Comitatus members now call themselves Sovereign Citizens. In recent years, the FBI along with local officials have arrested members of Sovereign Citizens in Arizona, Idaho, Utah, North Dakota, and Washington State for various crimes such as possessing illegal drugs, tax fraud, and filing fake liens against commercial properties.

Black Separatists

Although black separatists respond in part to centuries of white racism, as the SPLC asserts, they also "are strongly anti-white and anti-Semitic, and a number of religious versions assert that blacks—not Jews—are the Biblical 'chosen people' of God."[16] They also spout views like those of the Nation of Islam, whose leaders have falsely insisted that Jews are part of a conspiracy to gain world power, that Jews worship in a "synagogue of Satan," and that Jews have tried to destroy the black community.

White Nationalists

White nationalists believe in white supremacy and contend that nonwhites and Jews are inferior "mud races." In addition, the white nationalist movement is made up of a core of "three large groups . . . the Council of Conservative Citizens . . . that fights against school integration and racial intermarriage; *American Renaissance*, a journal that . . . [attacks] the intelligence and mental health of

It Happened to Lynx and Lamb Gaede

Twins Lynx and Lamb Gaede, pop singers, became famous in 2005 after they appeared on the *ABC News* show *20/20*. At the time they were featured because of their white nationalist beliefs and adoration of Adolf Hitler. As preteens, they once wore T-shirts with Hitler-like smiley faces and called themselves Prussian Blue. Raised on a California farm where their grandfather branded his cattle and horse with a swastika, they were homeschooled by their mother, April Gaede, "who has been a prominent member of racist fringe groups like the National Alliance and the National Vanguard." She "brought up her daughters with the ethos of white nationalism—a mix of racial pride, anti-immigrant hostility, Holocaust denial and resistance to the encroachment of 'muds,' i.e., Jews and nonwhites," wrote Aaron Gell for the *Daily*.[17]

The Gaedes moved to Montana and the twins enrolled in public schools, where apparently they began to change. They were out of the public eye for about five years because of illness. Lynx had cancer and Lamb has scoliosis. Those health problems and a realization that they no longer believed in white nationalism prompted the twins to come forth publicly, granting several interviews. At age nineteen, the twins contended they were not the kind of teens that they once presented to the public. "I'm grown up now. I was a little kid back then and said a lot of things I don't believe in now," Lynx told *ABC News* in 2011.[18] "We just want to come from a place of love and light," Lamb said. "I think we're meant to do something more—we're healers. We just want to exert the most love and positivity we can."[19]

black people; and the American Third Position (A3P), a racist party with electoral ambition," the SPLC reports.[20]

Patriot Movement

The SPLC identified 1,274 antigovernment "Patriot" groups that were active in 2011. Of these groups, 334 were militias, or civilian military forces. The Patriots had their start in 1994, and according to Mark Potok of SPLC, the movement initially was "a response to what was seen as violent government repression of dissident groups at Ruby Ridge, Idaho, in 1992 and near Waco, Texas, in 1993 along with anger at gun control and the Democratic Clinton administration in general."[21]

Ruby Ridge in the mountain area near the Canadian border is where white supremacist Randy Weaver and his family settled in a crude mountain cabin with no electricity or telephone. The Weavers had attended neo-Nazi meetings and held Christian Identity beliefs, but did not appear to be a threat to anyone. Randy Weaver had been arrested for selling illegal firearms to federal undercover agents but was released on his own recognizance. He was supposed to appear in court on the weapons charges. But he did not show up because he had not received word about the date for his appearance. In August 1992 federal officials prepared to arrest Weaver again. As federal agents tried to get close to the Weavers' cabin, one law enforcement officer shot the family's dog, precipitating a gun fight that killed Weaver's wife, Vicki, and fourteen-year-old son, Sammy. William Degan, a deputy U.S. marshal, was also killed. Randy Weaver was captured, tried, and sentenced to eighteen months in jail. After his release, Randy Weaver moved back to his hometown in "Iowa with his children and filed a wrongful death lawsuit against the government for the killing of Samuel and Vicki Weaver. In an out-of-court settlement, Randy was given $100,000 and his daughters were granted $1 million apiece," wrote David Lohr.[22]

The Waco, Texas, incidents in 1993 involved a cult compound known as the Branch Davidians headed by David Koresh. Like Weaver, Koresh was wanted on weapons charges. Federal agents tried to persuade Koresh to surrender. After a fifty-one-day siege by federal agents, Branch Davidian disciples set fire to the compound. Koresh and eighty-five of his followers, including young children, died in the inferno.

Many Americans were convinced that Koresh and his cult were responsible for their own deaths, although federal agents admitted they had made mistakes. Radical antigovernment groups such as the Patriots believed federal agents had committed murder, which is what they believed happened with the Weaver family.

According to some news accounts, the Ruby Ridge and Waco assaults were a catalyst for the 1995 bombing of the Alfred R. Murrah Federal Building in Oklahoma City, Oklahoma, where 168 people died and hundreds were injured. Timothy McVeigh and Terry Nichols were arrested in connection with the crime. The two were adamantly antigovernment. McVeigh was especially influenced by *The Turner Diaries*, a 1978 novel by neo-Nazi William Pierce, who describes how to blow up a FBI building and begin a war against the U.S. government. The bombing apparently was related to the fact that the U.S. Bureau of Alcohol, Tobacco, Firearms, and Explosives had an office in the building. McVeigh was executed for the crime in 2001; Nichols was sentenced to life in prison.

By 1996 the Patriot movement had peaked. At that time there were 858 groups. By 2000, the number of Patriot groups totaled less than 150. But membership in the movement increased in late 2008, when the economy declined and "Barack Obama appeared on the political scene as the Democratic nominee and, ultimately, the president-elect," Potok reports.[23]

Militant Militias

Some Patriot groups and members of Sovereign Citizens have connections with or are members of militant militias. Militias have been part of America ever since colonial days—long before the war for independence from Britain. During the

Chalk It Up to "Frightening Rhetoric"

In 2012, students at Towson University in Baltimore, Maryland, held a forum to discuss white-pride messages chalked on sidewalks around the campus, where it is a common practice to post information about university events on the sidewalks. But the chalking upset Kenan Herbert, a senior at the university and president of the Black Student Union. Herbert told a reporter, "As a black student, those words scared and concerned me. A lot of other students and I feel unsafe with this organization being on campus."[24]

Youth for Western Civilization (YWC) accepted responsibility for the chalkings. Since its founding in 2006, the YWC says its mission is to "educate, organize and train activists on campuses across the nation." The former president of YWC, Matthew Heimbach, declared that the YWC was "only promoting traditional conservative values and is not racist." He also told the *Baltimore Sun* that he is "advocating pride in his culture," and not white power.[25]

However, the YWC no longer exists at Towson University because its adviser ended his affiliation with the group. The former adviser, Professor Richard Vatz, said, "Frightening rhetoric" and unsophisticated vehemence of YWC are "not how impressive and serious conservatives argue their case."[26] Without an adviser, YWC cannot be officially recognized as a student group.

American Revolution, colonies organized armed citizen groups to be prepared to fight against the British if necessary. After independence and adoption of the Constitution, the states were given the authority to train and discipline these armed groups. More than a century later, in 1903, the militias were organized into one unit as the National Guard, independent of the regular army. In 1916, the National Guard became a reserve unit of the army. The federal government equips and funds the National Guard along with the Air National Guard. States and territories may also have their own defense forces or militias that are regulated by state laws.

Militant right-wing militias are not the same as the National Guard or state defense forces. Rather they are unofficial civilian organizations, and most states have passed laws to regulate or prohibit these groups. Along with Patriots and Sovereign Citizens, armed militias believe the U.S. government is their enemy and that there is a Jewish conspiracy to control the world—both false ideas. They also join other conspiracy theorists in believing the following:

- Federal agents in black helicopters are flying across the United States, spying on citizens.
- The federal government is preparing for a New World Order and a takeover of the country by the United Nations.
- Various types of foreign troops are being trained in secret U.S. sites.
- News media refuse to inform the American people about the conspiracy information that the militia has gathered.
- The federal government is controlling the weather in order to destroy people and property.
- The federal government has built large concentration camps to hold American dissidents.

Spreading Lies and Hate

For decades neo-Nazis, Patriots, black separatists, white nationalists, and other groups have spread their propaganda and hate messages through the print media—pamphlets, newsletters, books, and other published materials. One of the oldest manuscripts used by U.S. hate groups is the notorious anti-Semitic forgery *The Protocols of the Elders of Zion* that stemmed from a centuries-old myth about worldwide Jewish control of the monetary system and politics. Apparently *The Protocols* was written in the 1890s by members of the Russian secret police who claimed that a Jewish council planned to destroy Christianity and control the world. The work was widely distributed in Europe and the United States during the 1920s and 1930s, and it is still extensively circulated in the Middle East and Arab countries. The fabricated account became the standard way to justify Nazism and anti-Semitism.

Some prominent Americans—such as pilot Charles Lindbergh, known for making the first solo flight across the Atlantic Ocean, and Henry Ford, the automobile manufacturer—embraced the ideas in *The Protocols*. Ford financed the *Dearborn Independent*, a newspaper that published a series of articles he wrote or helped write, perpetuating the myth about a worldwide Jewish conspiracy.

Radio, television, videos, and telephones have been other common media for communicating hate. Consider Father Charles Coughlin, a Michigan-based Roman Catholic cleric, whose extremely popular 1930s radio program routinely attracted up to forty million listeners. Coughlin established an independent weekly titled *Social Justice*, which reprinted excerpts from *The Protocols of the Elders of Zion*. In his weekly newspaper and in broadcasts, Coughlin charged that some Jews had been communist leaders and/or controlled financial industries. How people of Jewish background could be communists and capitalists simultaneously is questionable at best. But Coughlin continued with his accusations until the archbishop of Detroit, Edward Mooney, ordered Coughlin to stop his political activities; if he did not comply, Coughlin would be relieved of his ministerial duties. Coughlin obeyed his superior and continued as a parish priest until he retired in 1966.

Graffiti on walls, buildings, vehicles, and infrastructures are other ways that groups and individuals spread hate messages. In 2011, racist graffiti was painted on a restroom wall at Seaholm High School in Birmingham, Michigan. The graffiti targeted five black students, including senior Courtney Isaiah Thomas, who reported to school authorities that the words "should be lynched" and "I'm going to kill them" were scribbled beside his and the other black students' names. After questioning by police, Thomas admitted that he was responsible for the false graffiti. Although it is not certain what he hoped to accomplish with the graffiti, one contributing factor might have been to imply that a white student was responsible. Earlier in the year a white student had repeatedly bullied Thomas, which might have affected him, his attorney noted. Thomas was suspended from school and was "arraigned in the 48th District Court on one count of ethnic intimidation. It is a felony offense punishable by two years in prison," *BET.com* reported.[27] However, in a plea bargain, the intimidation charge was dropped. Thomas agreed to plead guilty to a lesser charge of disorderly conduct. He was sentenced to one year of probation and one hundred hours of community service.

In today's world, modern communication systems can spread hate propaganda and outright lies in minutes. It is easy to call a radio station or TV channel and repeat an outlandish rumor such as a truckload of guillotines will be used to behead Patriots. Believing that is like believing Santa Claus is Satan in disguise.

However, for hate groups the quickest way to spread their messages is the electronic media, from e-mail to social networking to texting to websites. Anyone

Members of hate groups often express themselves by yelling racial and ethnic slurs at people who appear different from themselves.

who accesses Facebook, YouTube, or similar sites can find groups or individuals spewing their despicable words, cartoons, and other graphics. You can also be redirected to a hate site when you are trying to find information about a benign topic or to complete a school project, for example.

The online newspaper *Huffington Post* reported in 2011 that New York City high school students using Google began searching online for material about Martin Luther King Jr. to complete an assignment. One site they encountered was martinlutherking.org (or mlking.org or mlking.com). The site is operated by white supremacists who denigrate King and accuse him of being a communist, immoral character, wife beater, and phony. As Keith Thompson noted on the *Huffington Post*, little can be done to get the fake site off the Internet because of "multiple obstacles, not least of which is the First Amendment. Unless the Web content contains libel, a credible threat or incitement to imminent lawless action, the law offers little recourse."[28]

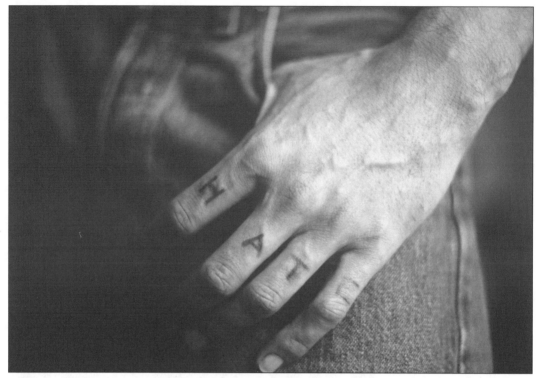

Tattoos are one way that hate messages are conveyed, although the word hate on this man's fingers is mild compared to the graphics inked on white supremacists and neo-Nazis.

Anonymous Hackers

An international collective known as Anonymous is hacking hate group websites to disable them. In January 2012, the hackers launched what they call Operation Blitzkrieg. Blitzkrieg, meaning "lightning war," was the term for a German tactic involving speed and surprise used in World War II. According to *Examiner.com* Anonymous hackers "released member information from the far-right National Democratic Party (NPD), the major neo-Nazi party in Germany. In addition to making public the identity of NPD supporters and donors, Anonymous also released internal NPD emails. The action shut down 15 websites linked to Germany's neo-Nazi National Democratic Party, including one far right platform called Altermedia."[29]

Throughout 2012, Anonymous hackers as well as an offshoot called Lulz-Financial went after the websites of other groups, such as the white supremacist Stormfront, anti-immigrant state governments (Alabama, for one), child pornography sites, and the Westboro Baptist Church that demonstrates at military funerals with signs like "Thank God for IEDs" and also demonstrates with antigay signs such as "God Hates Fags."

One basic hacker attack is denial of service. That is, a large number of computers access websites with bogus requests for information. The assault causes the site to temporarily blackout. Another tactic is to publicize personal information—names, addresses, cell phone numbers, credit card information, and the like—of a site's members.

Although hackers can shut down hate-group sites for a time, the sites usually are restored within a short period. But the most damage comes from revealing the names of those who support hate groups. These people do not want to be known publicly because they could be at risk of losing their jobs or face other types of economic backlash.

In spite of well-intentioned actions to disrupt hate groups, hackers face investigations by international, federal, state, and local law enforcement. It is a criminal offense to access a website without authorization to modify or deform it. And in 2011 and 2012, authorities arrested dozens of hackers in the United States and Europe. International raids in 2012 also brought arrests of twenty-five hackers in Chile, Argentina, Columbia, and Spain. Nevertheless, arrests have not stopped hackers intent on disrupting hate group websites, even those with high security. Savvy hackers have been able to invade supposedly secure government sites, so they are likely to keep attacking hate groups successfully.

Notes

1. Erik Maza, "Towson University Student Group's Messages Spark Debate over Racism," *Baltimore Sun*, March 9, 2012, articles.baltimoresun.com/2012-03-09/news/bs-md-towson-protest-20120309-22_1_student-group-towson-university-student-white-pride (accessed June 7, 2012).
2. Mary Elizabeth Williams, "Who Hires a Hate Group to Lead a School Assembly?" *Salon.com*, March 16, 2012, www.salon.com/2012/03/16/who_hires_a_hate_group_to_lead_a_school_assembly/ (accessed May 23, 2012).
3. Dennis Magee, "'Prophet' Eyes a Second Visit to Dunkerton," *WCFCourier.com*, March 12, 2012, wcfcourier.com/news/local/prophet-eyes-a-second-visit-to-dunkerton/article_159e75de-6af4-5527-93d6-54ec9614d8e7.html (accessed May 23, 2012).
4. Williams, "Who Hires a Hate Group to Lead a School Assembly?"
5. Marcia Barlow, *United Families International Guide to Family Issues: Sexual Orientation*, n.d., 7, unitedfamilies.org/downloads/Sex.pdf (accessed May 24, 2012).
6. Igor Volsky, ThinkProgress, September 9, 2011, thinkprogress.org/lgbt/2011/09/09/315816/opponent-of-californias-gay-ed-law-gays-are-kidnapping-the-brains-of-the-kids/ (accessed May 24, 2012).
7. Sons of Thundr website, www.sonsofthundr.com/sodomitescanbesaved.html (accessed May 24, 2012).
8. *Failed Messiah* (blog), failedmessiah.typepad.com/failed_messiahcom/2011/10/haredi-fringe-group-claims-molestation-of-boys-has-surged-since-same-sex-marriage-bill-passed-in-ny-345.html (accessed May 24, 2012).

9. Linda Harvey, "Teaching Our Youth about Homosexuality and Gender Identity," Mission: America, n.d., www.missionamerica.com/index.php (accessed May 24, 2012).

10. Stephen D. Foster, "Anti-Gay Pastor Claims That Half of All Murders in Cities Are Committed by Homosexuals," Addicting Info, November 16, 2011, www.addictinginfo .org/2011/11/16/anti-gay-pastor-claims-that-half-of-all-murders-in-cities-are-committed -by-homosexuals/ (accessed May 24, 2012).

11. Prophet Walker, "The Anti-Christ . . . His Synagogue," *The True Light* (blog), January 19, 2012, onenesschristian.blogspot.com/ (accessed May 24, 2012).

12. Josh Israel, "Newly Designated Anti-Gay Hate Groups Earned That Distinction," Think-Progress, March 9, 2012, thinkprogress.org/lgbt/2012/03/09/441448/anti-gay-hate-groups -earned-that-distinction/ (accessed May 23, 2012).

13. Jackie Alexander, "Eastside Students Learn about Racism, Yesterday and Today," *Gainesville .com*, February 22, 2012, www.gainesville.com/article/20120222/ARTICLES/120229799 ?template=printart (accessed June 5, 2012).

14. Alexander, "Eastside Students Learn about Racism."

15. Maxine D. Jones, principal investigator, et al., *Documented History of the Incident Which Occurred at Rosewood, Florida in January 1923*, submitted to the Florida Board of Regents, December 22, 1993, www.displaysforschools.com/rosewoodrp.html (accessed June 4, 2012).

16. Southern Poverty Law Center, "Black Separatist," n.d., www.splcenter.org/get-informed/ intelligence-files/ideology/black-separatist (accessed May 26, 2012).

17. Aaron Gell, "Change of Heart," *Daily*, July 17, 2011, www.thedaily.com/page/2011/07/17/ 071711-news-nazi-twins-1-6/ (accessed August 28, 2012).

18. Juju Chang, "Teen Twins Lamb and Lynx Gaede Deny Neo-Nazi Past, Say 'It Was a Job,'" *ABC News*, July 21, 2011, abcnews.go.com/US/teen-twins-lamb-lynx-gaede-deny-neo-nazi/ story?id=14124412#.T7_RtVJ61ac (accessed May 28, 2012).

19. Gell, "Change of Heart."

20. Mark Potok, "The Year in Hate and Extremism," *Intelligence Report*, Spring 2012, 42.

21. Potok, "The Year in Hate and Extremism," 39.

22. David Lohr, "All about Randy Weaver and Ruby Ridge," truTV.com, n.d., www.trutv.com/ library/crime/gangsters_outlaws/cops_others/randy_weaver/21.html (accessed May 29, 2012).

23. Potok, "The Year in Hate and Extremism," 39.

24. Maza, "Towson University Student Group's Messages Spark Debate over Racism."

25. Hatewatch staff, "YWC Members Chalk 'White Pride' on University Sidewalks," *Hatewatch/ Southern Poverty Law Center* (blog), March 13, 2012, www.splcenter.org/blog/2012/03/13/ ywc-members-chalk-white-pride-on-university-sidewalks/print/ (accessed May 31, 2012).

26. Imagine 2050 editors, "Youth for Western Civilization Dismantled at Towson University," Imagine 2050, March 29, 2012, imagine2050.newcomm.org/2012/03/29/youth-for-western -civilization-dismantled-at-towson-university/ (accessed May 31, 2012).

27. Frank McCoy, "Black Michigan Teen Is Charged with Ethnic Intimidation," *BET.com*, May 18, 2011, www.bet.com/news/national/2011/05/18/black-michigan-teen-is-charged-with -ethnic-intimidation.html (accessed August 28, 2012).

28. Keith Thompson, "White Supremacist Site MartinLutherKing.org Marks 12th Anniversary," *Huffington Post*, January 16, 2011, www.huffingtonpost.com/keith-thomson/white-supremacist -site-ma_b_809755.html?view=print&comm_ref=false (accessed June 4, 2012).

29. Michael Stone, "Anonymous Hits KKK Website: Operation Blitzkreig Continues," *Examiner .com*, May 28, 2012, www.examiner.com/article/anonymous-hits-kkk-website-operation -blitzkrieg-continues (accessed June 5, 2012).

NO TIME FOR HATE

"Overcoming my personal struggle with bullying and loneliness inspired me to create WeStopHate . . . a non-profit program changing the way teens view themselves by collectively helping ourselves and each other accept, embrace, and love who we are."—Seventeen-year-old Emily-Anne Rigal[1]

Reducing hate, bigotry, and intolerance usually begins with personal attitudes such as those expressed by Emily-Anne Rigal and by exploring how one feels toward those who appear different or act in a different way from oneself. People who have low self-esteem and feel threatened by differences or who need the security of group acceptance may have problems appreciating differences—whether it's skin color, religion, gender, income, physical shape or size, or mental capabilities. On the other hand, people with a strong sense of self-worth usually are well aware that each of us is unique in her or his way. Emily-Anne notes that WeStopHate focuses on teen esteem because "only when we see a rise in self-esteem, will we see a decline in bullying. This is because people who are happy with themselves won't put others down."[2]

Individuals and groups in many parts of the United States have initiated programs to counteract hate, bigotry, and intolerance. Some, such as WeStopHate, focus on ways to prevent bullying and to support those who have been bullied. Another such program is Stop the Hate, Spread the Hope, a teenage group in Onondaga County, New York. Nick Longo, one of the organizers, says the group wants to talk to people about bullying and what can be done to stop it.[3]

Youth Ambassadors, chosen by the STOMP Out Bullying program, know what it's like to be bullied and work on a variety of projects to stop bullying, such as the Blue Shirt Day—World Day of Bullying Prevention in schools. In addition, ambassadors—most of them teenagers—have created antibullying books and videos, worked on antidrug campaigns, volunteered for programs to stop child abuse, raised funds for charity organizations, served on antidrinking campaigns, and are community leaders. They come from states ranging from New York to Wyoming, and their stories are online at www.stompoutbullying.org/youth_advisors.php.

Along with antibullying campaigns, numerous individuals and groups try to reduce the bigotry aimed at religious, ethnic, and racial groups. Local, state, and federal government agencies are also involved in such efforts. An example is the National Hate Crime Prevention Project, funded jointly by the U.S. Department of Justice's Office of Juvenile Justice and Delinquency Prevention and the U.S. Department of Education's Safe and Drug Free Schools Program. The media—print, electronic, and broadcast—also have presented features that alert the public to hate mongers and ways to deal with bigots and racists.

"Not in Our Town"

In 1995, the Public Broadcasting Service (PBS) aired a special that depicted a project in Billings, Montana, called Not in Our Town, which began in 1993. That year after racist and anti-Semitic graffiti were sprayed on hilltop rocks above the city, Police Chief Wayne Inman ordered city workers to paint over the hate messages. But the graffiti appeared again and again along with racist leaflets distributed across town. As the hate messages escalated, the community became concerned and began to organize to prevent violence and to help victims of attacks. For example, when skinheads invaded an African American Methodist Episcopal church to intimidate the congregation, members of predominantly white churches began to attend the black church to lend support. When a cement block was thrown through the window of a Jewish home where a menorah was displayed, the local newspaper published a full-page picture of a menorah. With encouragement from the newspaper, thousands of Jews and non-Jews displayed the picture in their windows as a sign of unity.

The PBS broadcast in 1995 about the Billings project precipitated campaigns across the United States to prevent bigotry and hate crimes. Not in Our Town has spawned other projects that are currently active, such as Not on Our Campus, Not in Our Halls, Not in Our School—all of which try to counteract hate, bigotry, and intolerance. In June 2012, the city of Marshalltown, Iowa, for example, launched its Not-in-Our-Town effort to stop bullying in schools, workplaces, and homes (focusing on domestic violence). Also, when the Westboro Baptist Church group planned to visit Olympia High School on June 7, 2012, in Washington State, Olympia students, parents, and staff organized Not in Our School. Students held a unity rally called Oly (for Olympia) Love to counteract the Westboro group, and seventeen pastors signed a letter sent to the church, which clearly stated that the pastors believe Westboro Baptists "do not reflect the heart and mind of Christ as revealed in the Bible; nor are they an accurate reflection of how the Bible describes a follower of Christ." While the Westboro group claims to have a Biblical basis for their rhetoric, their message is clearly adverse to many

A handshake is still a friendly gesture and a step toward reducing hate.

passages from the Bible. And the pastors' letter concludes that Westboro Baptists "do not speak for us."[4]

Anytown

Anytown is not really a town. Rather it is a week-long summer camp created by the National Conference of Community and Justice (NCCJ) for a diverse group of teenagers. The camps are held in numerous states, and participants—known as Delegates—attend the camp to learn how "to become effective, responsible global leaders and community builders." According to NCCJ, high school students "come together to build a community based on respect, understanding, and inclusivity." The Anytown website for Connecticut and Western Massachusetts further notes,

> Through interactive games, workshops, and discussions, Delegates, along with staff members explore the thoughts, opinions and experiences we all share on topics like prejudice, discrimination, and hate. Through this dialogue, the Delegates are taken on a journey to create a model for an ideal community in which members not just tolerate, but celebrate each other's

differences. It is the goal of ANYTOWN to equip the Delegates with the knowledge and skills to transform their home communities into places where individual differences are seen as positive tools that bring people together instead of keeping them apart.[5]

Teenager Silvana attended the camp in 2009 when she was in eleventh grade. She reported that she listened to other delegates and "was able to . . . see how things such as racism, sexism, heterosexism, oppression and prejudice affect them in their day to day life. . . . I was surprised to see how well I could relate to the new friends that surrounded me."[6]

Marquis from Windsor High School noted, "Experiences that have come from Anytown are impossible to overlook. I made countless friendships with people of all races, economic backgrounds, sexual orientations and religions. There is such a diverse collection of people. Anytowners formed a rapport . . . by conferring on outlooks, bigotry and incidents when we felt that we were the object of hate."[7]

Charles had this to report:

Prior to camp, I saw segregation occurring around me daily. I observed black kids sitting together at lunch and white kids hanging out with each other in hallways, but never really did much about it. I tried to surround myself with different types of people, and still do today, but besides that I never really tried to make a change. In fact, today I would classify myself more as "part of the problem" then [sic] the "solution." I thought it was cool to call things "retarded" and even laughed when my friends said some pretty racist things. ANYTOWN completely changed that aspect of me.[8]

Brishell's comments seem to sum up what Anytown is about:

Experiencing what others faced in the past and going through these activities really impacted my perception of our society. Now more than ever, I believe that everyone should be equal and be respected. Having had the opportunity to "walk in someone else's shoes," I think differently and feel that instead of solving the bigger problems first, we should begin with the little ones. Problems that may seem minor are the ones that build up to bigger ones and if it is possible to get rid of them, then maybe someday there can be peace and equality.[9]

Students Protest Racism and Bigotry

"Posters, slogans and banners won't erase the prejudices of a bigot, but they will make an ignorant teenager stop and think about how their words affect other people. Prejudice isn't a swastika on a whiteboard or a friend dropping the word 'gay' but ignorance is. The way to combat ignorance is to educate," wrote Deidre Ratliff in a 2011 edition of *Michigan Daily*, the campus newspaper of the University of Michigan at Ann Arbor. A junior at the university, Ratliff has been part of an antibias campaign on campus to educate students about the hurtful effect of bigoted messages. She admits, "A campus committee isn't going to solve prejudice on Michigan's campus. But I shudder to think of what would happen if every campaign decided it was better to do nothing than try something, no matter how small."[10]

Justice Namaste, junior at Williamsville East High School in Buffalo, New York, agrees with that sentiment. Writing for *Buffalo News* in 2011, Justice noted,

> As a teenager, I've found that we, as a generation, have a lot to say. Granted, not all of it is worth saying, but we put it out there anyway. . . . When it comes to speaking up against something that's wrong, whether it is blatant, physical bullying or merely a friend saying "That's so gay," many of us remain silent. It's easy to sign anti-bullying pledges . . . but actually being the one person who stands up and says, "No, that's wrong" is a whole different story.[11]

Eighteen-year-old Christian Collins, who is on the staff of *VOX*, a newspaper created by and for teens in Atlanta, Georgia, wrote that she is going to do her small part to try to stop racist language. As she explained in an essay,

> If my mother stood in the hallway at my school listening to my friends greet each other she would be shocked. "What's up, my nigga?" and "How you living, my nigga?" This racial slur is now fondly spewed from the mouths of today's youth to show affection. I see the word as being destructive, and yes, I'm guilty of using it. But . . . I'm permanently eras[ing] the word from my vocabulary. . . .
>
> The word will always have a derogatory meaning and tone. The frequency of the word being used in pop culture is alarming to me. . . . The power of words can be startling. The menace and hatred behind the N-word causes pain. . . . To honor our black roots, we must progress. But progression means leaving behind the word that has haunted us for so long. Let's find a new way to show affection for each other. I, and I hope others, will let go of a word that is continually used to disrespect and degrade us.[12]

In February 2012, student Krystal Myers at Lenoir City High School in Tennessee staged a protest through *knoxnews.com*. Myers is an honors student, captain of the swim team, and editor of her high school newspaper, *Panther Press*. She is also an atheist and had written an editorial for the student paper titled "No Rights: The Life of an Atheist." Her editorial begins with the comment, "I feel that my rights as an atheist are severely limited when compared to other students who are Christians." She points out,

> Not only are there multiple clubs featuring the Christian faith, but youth ministers are also allowed to come onto the school campus and hand candy and other food out to Christians and their friends. However, I feel like if an atheist did that, people would not be happy about it. This may not be true, but because of pervasive negative feelings towards atheists in the school, I feel that it would be the case. My question is, "Why? Why does atheism have such a bad reputation?" And an even better question: "Why do Christians have special rights not allowed to nonbelievers?"[13]

Also she noted numerous examples of "pro-Christian" activities at the school, such as prayer at graduation ceremonies and athletic events, which are unconstitutional, Myers declared. For example, she noted coaches encourage prayer before a swim meet, which she did not want to be part of but felt forced to do so as captain of the swim team. School officials would not allow Myers to publish her editorial, so she went to the *Knox News Sentinel*, which posted it online.

Students at Catholic DeLaSalle High School in Minneapolis staged a protest in April 2012 during a presentation by the Archdiocese of St. Paul and Minneapolis. Representatives of the archdiocese—a priest and a Catholic couple—spoke about marriage at a mandatory school assembly for seniors. According to reporter Jon Tevlin, student Matt Bliss said,

> The first three-quarters of the presentation were really good. They talked about what is marriage and how marriage helps us as a society. Then . . . they started talking about single parents and adopted kids. They didn't directly say it, but they implied that kids who are adopted or live with single parents are less than kids with two parents of the opposite sex. They implied that a "normal" family is the best family. When they finally got to gay marriage, [students] were really upset. . . . You could look around the room and feel the anger. My friend who is a lesbian started crying, and people were crying in the bathroom.[14]

When the presenters compared homosexuality to bestiality, several students spoke out in disbelief and anger. One girl held up a sign saying, "I love my two moms," according to reporter Tevlin. Hannah, a student who is adopted, was upset because the representatives declared that adopted kids were "socially unstable," which she said was "hurtful." Unfortunately, the assembly did not end well—the priest and school officials cut off the student questions and left.[15]

At Furman University in Greenville, South Carolina, the Muslim Student Association (MSA) held a protest in March 2012 to counter what they described as "the hateful rhetoric employed against Muslims" by controversial speaker Nonie Darwish, an Egyptian American and former Muslim. She has been called "a staple of the Right-wing anti-Muslim Islamaphobia network,"[16] and students at other universities (University of New Mexico and University of California, Berkeley, are examples) have protested her speeches. At Furman, Darwish was sponsored by Conservative Students for a Better Tomorrow (CSBT) and was asked to speak on "Cruel and Unusual: Islamic Law, Women, and Minority Rights." However, the MSA objected to Darwish's appearance, as junior Hammad Khan pointed out in Furman's school newspaper, the *Paladin*. Darwish wrote, "Those who take time to read the Qur'an and Hadith and want to follow the example of Muhammad cannot help but be terrorists." Khan countered, "The dehumanization . . . of an entire religious tradition, the perpetuation of stereotypes, and the hateful rhetoric employed against Muslims in this statement is appalling."

Khan along with other members of the MSA held a peaceful protest outside the place where Darwish spoke. "Other Furman students supported MSA's efforts against bigotry and hateful rhetoric," Khan wrote. "The protest was not against Mrs. Darwish's or CSBT's freedom of speech—a right we all cherish and protect. It was against the discrepancy between the CLP [Cultural Life Program] mission and values and the evident lack of educational value of the event, the bigotry and the hateful rhetoric of the speaker."[17]

Students at Cesar Chavez Academy (CCA), a combined middle school and high school in Detroit, Michigan, held another type of protest in May 2012. They were part of a teen and youth organization called the Coalition to Defend Affirmative Action, Integration and Immigrants Rights and Fight for Equality by Any Means Necessary (BAMN). Two hundred students walked out of CCA even though teachers and administrators tried to stop them with threats of suspension and by physically blocking the doors and gates. Monica Smith, a spokesperson, gave one reason for the protest: "A racist white teacher at CCA named Nicole Szymberski . . . denigrated students heritage by speaking low of Mexican families, called at least one black student a 'black monkey' and told girl students 'the bigger the hoops the bigger the ho.'" When a Latino staff member spoke up for the students, he was fired.

The students continued their protest outside the school. As Monica explained, "BAMN is about doing what ever [*sic*] is necessary to ensure that we do not have to attend schools in which we are degraded for our Latina/o, black or any other culture, race, gender or sexual orientation. We will walkout, occupy, sit-in, march, rally and more to assert our power and win our demands." One small victory for the protestors: "The high school students were not suspended at all and the middle school students were suspended for one day only and no one was expelled." They planned to continue their fight "for full rights for immigrants, access to equal, quality schools and to have a first class city to live and grow in."[18]

A week after graduating from Maine's Kennebunk High School in June 2012, Silas Phipps-Costin posted a message on *Seacoastonline.com* to protest teacher Sean Watson's graduation address. Phipps-Costin called it "the most thinly veiled hate speech I have ever heard from an individual in a position of authority." He added,

> I heard a white, middle-class male spend close to a minute comparing equal opportunity and civil rights act to arranged marriages, and making racist and homophobic jokes about people being forced to marry other races or people of the same gender. . . . Mr. Watson is a teacher. Every day, dozens of students must interact with him in his classroom. Many of those students belong to the groups he attacked—minority students and LGBTQ [lesbian, gay, bisexual, transgender, and queer] students. I cannot imagine a way that any gay or black student could possibly feel safe in the classroom of a teacher who has publicly stated he thinks it is "unfair" to protect them from discrimination.[19]

The graduate's comments were followed by an editorial and another article that included Watson's complete address. While speaking to students Watson said in part, "I'm arguing that affirmative action is unfair to bigots, and even bigots have a right to be treated fairly. . . . I disapprove, and I hope every one of you disapproves of bigotry. But the private virtue of tolerance and the public virtue of tolerance require us to tolerate things, which we do not approve. (This speech perhaps.)"[20]

The editorial in *Seacoastonline* supported Watson's free-speech right to present his address, but opined that the teacher owed graduates an apology for "upsetting and offending many" in the class of 2012.[21]

What You Can Do

Many pamphlets, brochures, and websites have helpful information for individuals who want do something to help stop bigotry, intolerance, and racism. Individuals nationwide and around the world take actions against bigotry and racism by joining grassroots groups working to overcome intolerant behavior. Some people may choose to participate in street drama, concerts, plays, art shows, and other events that call attention to civil rights violations and discrimination. Others may study cultures different from their own (even learning another language) in

It Happened at Newcomers High School

Newcomers High School in Queens, New York, is a school for new immigrants, and it is a place where students from varied countries are enrolled. Because of the many attacks—verbal and physical—against immigrants in recent years, Julie Mann, a teacher at Newcomers, and eighth grade teacher Kim Allen at St. Luke's School, an Episcopal school in Greenwich Village, worked together to try to diminish stereotypes of immigrants. St. Luke's students take part each year in research on immigration, and they helped edit the immigrant narratives for a digital presentation. The result is an online publication titled *Building Bridges, Telling Our Stories*, which includes accounts of teenage immigrants from Albania, Bangladesh, Brazil, China, Colombia, Congo, Ecuador, Haiti, Indonesia, Ivory Coast, Poland, Russia, and Tibet.

Eighteen-year-old Arefa Akter from Bangladesh explains in her story,

In Bangladesh we do not have human rights for all people. People are abused in many ways, women most of all. Women are restricted by men, who always try to control women. Men think that women do not need an education or a job. Most of them have religious barriers and believe in superstitions because they want women to stay home. Women cannot go outside, or shop. If they do go out, they have to cover their whole body.

Akter relates that she came to the United States "for a better education and to have a better life and have a better future. In my country we do not have access to a good education."[22]

Jonnathan Arias, age eighteen, came to the United States from Ecuador. His parents had immigrated while Jonnathan was a youngster, leaving him with grandparents and other relatives in Ecuador. He was able to join his family when he was sixteen. In his account, he declares,

Something that I want to say about immigration is that it doesn't matter where people come from, it doesn't matter what religion you are, it doesn't matter what skin color you have or whether you are an undocumented person in this country. We are the same: we are humans and all of us have the same rights which must be respected. We all came to this country with the intention of working very hard to have a good life and build a better future for our children.[23]

Nineteen-year-old Jie Yu is from China, and his story concludes the 132-page publication. He lives in New York City and like the other storytellers attends Newcomers High School. In his account he notes,

In school I feel relaxed and equal. All the students—Chinese, Spanish, Indian and Haitian—we work together and respect and help each other. I also do community service. Almost every Saturday, I go to the Herald Mission center with my friend and volunteer to help people, to do the best for them. When I finish work I feel content and full of energy, even if I have had to stand the whole day.

Now that I live in America I appreciate and enjoy freedom, diversity, competition and peace. These factors have helped me to take root along with all the other people who have come to this country since it was established . . . as a land of immigrants. . . . I hope our country will always be a land where people's dreams come true and not a land that destroys people's dreams. When I am an independent adult, I want to help people. I want strive to make our beautiful country a place where everyone's dreams can come true.[24]

order to rid themselves of preconceived notions about an ethnic group, which in turn helps reduce bigotry and racism. Political activists might campaign or vote for candidates who support legislative actions to reduce bigotry and intolerance.

As an individual you might make a conscious effort to be involved in activities that include people of varied racial and ethnic groups. You might want to participate in an exchange program such as going with a group to visit a place of worship different from your own. Or taking part in Teaching Tolerance's Mix-It-Up program at lunchtime in the school cafeteria where students venture outside their segregated "comfort zone" to sit with classmates of another culture.

Off the Bookshelf

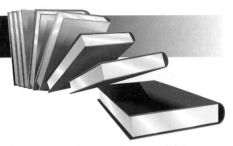

Author Julian Houston mixes actual events from the civil rights era (1950s and 1960s) with fictional accounts of the hero in his novel *New Boy*. Set in the late 1950s, the story depicts ways that racism and bigotry can be and are overcome. Teenager Rob Garrett leaves segregated Virginia to enter Draper, a boarding school in Connecticut. Rob's parents—both professionals—make the arrangements for him to go to the private school because they want him to "have the best education available." Rob is the first student of color in the school, and he begins his studies quietly with few problems. However, he discovers a kind of bigotry he had not expected when his two friends are targeted. His friend, Vinnie, is harassed repeatedly because he is Italian and also because of his severe acne. The final blow for Vinnie comes when his tormenters put a pile of dog feces in his laundry bag, forcing Vinnie out of the dormitory to the infirmary. Another friend, Gordie Burns, is ridiculed for being Jewish. Though publicly humiliated by some of his classmates, Gordie manages to stay calm. He explains to Rob that the fathers of the harassers give a lot of money to Draper, so officials do little to stop their bigoted incidents.

Gordie, who is from a wealthy family in New York City, invites Rob to his home during Thanksgiving vacation and the two make plans to visit jazz clubs even though they are underage. While in the city, Rob stays in Harlem with an aunt, a retired teacher, and he also goes out on his own, encountering Black Muslims and leader Malcolm X.

Much of the story is about Rob's experiences at school where he excels and makes the honor roll. But he is not satisfied at the school and at one time laments, "It's like being in a foreign country . . . you can't really be sure where you fit in because you don't speak the language and you don't know the people. . . . I keep thinking I should leave. I'm the only colored student in the whole school. They never had one of us before."[25]

Rob is torn by what is happening in his hometown. His friends and others are organizing for a sit-in at Woolworth's lunch counter in support of the widely publicized sit-in at a Woolworth's in Greensboro, North Carolina. Rob wants to be part of it. He manages to get a furlough from school and when the protest begins he and others hand out leaflets asking people to boycott the store. The protest gets ugly and whites attack some of the blacks at the lunch counter, severely injuring them. It is a turning point for Rob, who begins to face the life-threatening reality of bigotry and racism. But he does not react with hatred. Instead he decides his best course of action is to continue with his education at the boarding school.

One small but significant step was spelled out on the U.S. State Department's "2011 Hours against Hate" campaign to "stop bigotry and promote pluralism and respect across lines of culture, religion, tradition, class, and gender." On the site, viewers worldwide were asked to "pledge their time to stop hate—to do something for someone who doesn't look like you, pray like you, or live like you."[26]

Some other simple steps include signing petitions online or in person to protest bigotry and intolerance on talk radio or TV programs. Or joining a march to fight hate. Or carefully checking the sources of anti-Semitic, antihomosexual, antigovernment claims that appear on websites—are they from hate groups? Are the claims based on facts or myths?

The University of California, Santa Cruz, has posted "10 Ways to Fight Hate on Campus." Five of the suggestions in abbreviated form apply to individuals everywhere and are listed here:

1. Don't let hate go unchallenged. In cases of bullying, bystanders do just as much to contribute to the problem, because they enable the bully to use hatred to make other students think less of themselves. Step up.
2. Don't let hate tear people apart. . . . Pull together instead.
3. When hate strikes, don't remain silent. Join with others; use your voices to denounce bigotry.
4. Support the victims.
5. Teach tolerance.[27]

A helpful handbook on how to deal with intolerance, bigotry, and hate comes from the Southern Poverty Law Center. It's called *Speak Up!* and is full of dozens of ideas. In a section about family members who make racist jokes, one suggestion is to remind the speaker that the words are an unfair depiction, are offensive, and that such bigotry could create divisions in a family. The contents include the following sections: "What Can I Do about Sexist Remarks?" "What Can I Do about Racial Profiling?" "What Can I Do about Bias Bullying?" "What Can I Do about Retail Racism?" Retail racism refers to store clerks or security personnel who follow you or other customers. *Speak Up!* suggests, "Ask why the clerk or

Getting together with friends or classmates from varied ethnic and racial heritages is one way that bigotry and racism are reduced.

security officer is following you (or someone else). Ask to see the written policies on discrimination. Share your experience and observations with company officials." Another suggestion: "Stage a personal public protest. Go to the customer service desk or check-out counter. Cancel your store credit card on the spot, and say why you're doing so—loud enough for others to hear. Ask for the manager and tell that person the store has lost your business." A follow-up: "Let friends and family know what you observed or experienced. Encourage them to refrain from shopping at a store that practices racial profiling or to contact the store to ask about such policies and practices."[28]

A question that many people ask today is, What can I do about unwanted racist, sexist, or homophobic e-mail? One answer is to let the sender know you do not want that kind of e-mail, and if it is a forwarded ethnic joke, antireligious message, or cartoon, do not pass it on. A recent example received by this author is a photo of a dog's snout poking through a hole in a blanket with the caption "A guide dog for a Muslim woman." Underneath were the words "I do believe you call this a Barka." The sender thought this e-mail was "pretty funny," but it's doubtful a Muslim woman who wears a burka to abide by her religious beliefs would think it humorous.

For other ideas about what you can do to help prevent bigotry and intolerance, check out the handbook online at www.splcenter.org/sites/default/files/downloads/publication/SPLCspeak_up_handbook_0.pdf. As *Speak Up!* makes clear, one of the most effective measures one person can take is speaking out, a much-repeated suggestion. To remain silent may be seen as condoning intolerant and racist acts. You can refuse to listen to racist jokes, object to stereotyped labels, or simply say that you are offended by a racist or bigoted remark, whether or not that remark is directed at you.

In other words, to repeat another cliché: stand up and be counted!

Notes

1. Emily-Anne Rigal, "Creating a Movement to Stop Hate," *Huffington Post*, October 4, 2011, www.huffingtonpost.com/emilyanne-rigal/untitled_2_b_959042.html?view=print&comm_ref=false (accessed June 8, 2012).
2. Rigal, "Creating a Movement to Stop Hate."
3. Brad Vivacqua, "Stop the Hate, Spread the Hope," *YNN*, January 10, 2012, watertown.ynn.com/content/all_news/569696/stop-the-hate--spread-the-hope/ (accessed June 11, 2012).
4. Bruce, "Westboro 'Baptist Church' Is Coming to Our Town . . . a Public Statement from Olympia Area Pastors," CapitalVision.org, June 4, 2012, capitalvision.org/201206043991/westboro-baptist-church-is-coming-to-our-town-a-public-statement-from-olympia-area-pastors/ (accessed June 11, 2012).

5. National Conference for Community and Justice, "Anytown," n.d., www.nccj.org/whatwedo/anytown.html (accessed June 20, 2012).

6. Silvana, "My ANYTOWN Story," National Conference for Community and Justice, n.d., www.nccj.org/whatwedo/AnytownTestimonals.htm (accessed June 20, 2012).

7. Marquis, "My ANYTOWN Experience," National Conference for Community and Justice, n.d., www.nccj.org/whatwedo/AnytownTestimonals.htm (accessed June 20, 2012).

8. Charles, "My ANYTOWN Experience," National Conference for Community and Justice, n.d., www.nccj.org/whatwedo/AnytownTestimonals.htm (accessed June 20, 2012).

9. Brishell, "My ANYTOWN Experience," National Conference for Community and Justice, n.d., www.nccj.org/whatwedo/AnytownTestimonals.htm (accessed June 20, 2012).

10. Deidre Ratliff, "Letter to the Editor: Catchy Slogans Will Not Deter Campus Bigots," *Michigan Daily*, January 24, 2011, www.michigandaily.com/content/letter-editor-what-are-we-trying-accomplish (accessed June 14, 2012).

11. Justice Namaste, "Teenagers Need to Speak Up," *Buffalo News*, September 8, 2011, www.buffalonews.com/life/next/article548928.ece (accessed June 17, 2012).

12. Christian Collins, "The N-Word," *VOX*, May 5, 2012, www.voxteencommunications.org/essays/Story.aspx?ID=1699007 (accessed June 15, 2012).

13. Krystal Myers, "School Promotes Religion and Discrimination of Atheist Students," *knoxnews.com*, February 26, 2012, www.knoxnews.com/news/2012/feb/26/krystal-myers-school-promotes-religion-and-of/ (accessed June 16, 2012).

14. Jon Tevlin, "DeLaSalle Kids Have a Few Words with Archdiocese at Marriage Talk," *Star Tribune*, April 3, 2012, www.startribune.com/printarticle/?id=146031865 (accessed August 28, 2012).

15. Tevlin, "DeLaSalle Kids Have a Few Words with Archdiocese."

16. "Radical Anti-Muslim Islamophobe Nonie Darwish Invited to Speak at George Mason Law School," *Islamaphobia Today*, October 1, 2011, www.islamophobiatoday.com/2011/10/01/radical-anti-muslim-islamophobe-nonie-darwish-invited-to-speak-at-george-mason-law-school/ (accessed June 16, 2012).

17. Hammad Khan, "Bigotry on Campus," *Paladin*, March 22, 2012, www.thefurmanpaladin.com/opinions/bigotry-on-campus-1.2825880#.T9uFsph62So?compArticle=yes (accessed June 16, 2012).

18. Monica Smith, "March Today, March Tomorrow and Keep Fighting until We Win!" BAMN, June 5, 2012, www.bamn.com/immigrants-rights/victory-to-the-students-at-cesar-chavez-academy (accessed June 16, 2012).

19. Silas Phipps-Costin, "Teacher Needs to Publicly Apologize," *Seacoastonline.com*, June 21, 2012, www.seacoastonline.com/articles/20120621-OPINION-206210380 (accessed June 21, 2012).

20. Jennifer Feals, "Speech Sparks Debate," *Seacoastonline.com*, June 21, 2012, www.seacoastonline.com/articles/20120621-NEWS-206210367 (accessed June 21, 2012).

21. York County Coast Star, "Wrong Time, Place for Speech," *Seacoastonline.com*, June 12, 2012, www.seacoastonline.com/articles/20120621-OPINION-206210377 (accessed June 21, 2012).

22. Arefa Akter, "Telling My Story," ed. Alessandra Lampietti, *Building Bridges, Telling Our Stories* (2010–2011), 12, www.niot.org/sites/default/files/Newcomers_StudentPublication.pdf (accessed December 10, 2012).

23. Jonnathan Arias, "My Life As an Immigrant," ed. Luke Oldham, *Building Bridges, Telling Our Stories* (2010–2011), 16–17, www.niot.org/sites/default/files/Newcomers_Student Publication.pdf (accessed December 10, 2012).

24. Jie Yu, "American Dream," ed. Blythe Calderley, *Building Bridges, Telling Our Stories* (2010–2011), 132, www.niot.org/sites/default/files/Newcomers_StudentPublication.pdf (accessed December 10, 2012).

25. Julian Houston, *New Boy* (Boston, MA: Houghton Mifflin, 2005), 198–99.

26. Penny Starr, "State Department Uses Facebook to Fight 'against Hate' and 'Stop Bigotry'" *CNSNews.com*, November 22, 2011, cnsnews.com/news/article/state-department-uses-facebook-fight-against-hate-and-stop-bigotry (accessed June 18, 2012).

27. University of California, Santa Cruz, "10 Ways to Fight Hate on Campus," n.d., reporthate.ucsc.edu/resources/10-ways.html (accessed June 18, 2012).

28. Teaching Tolerance, *Speak Up!* (Montgomery, AL: Southern Poverty Law Center, n.d.), 72.

Selected Resources

Books

Anderson, Kristin J. *Benign Bigotry: The Psychology of Subtle Prejudice*. Cambridge, MA: Cambridge University Press, 2010.

Findley, Paul. *Speaking Out: A Congressman's Lifelong Fight against Bigotry, Famine, and War*. Chicago, IL: Lawrence Hill Books/imprint Chicago Review Press, 2011.

Kantor, Martin. *Homophobia: The State of Sexual Bigotry Today*. 2nd ed. Santa Barbara, CA: Praeger/imprint ABC-CLIO, 2009.

Kivel, Paul. *Uprooting Racism: How White People Can Work for Racial Justice*. Expanded 3rd ed. Gabriola Island, BC, Canada: New Society Publishers, 2011.

Levin, Jack A., and Jim Nolan. *The Violence of Hate: Confronting Racism, Anti-Semitism, and Other Forms of Bigotry*. 3rd ed. New York: Prentice Hall, 2010.

Peters, Shawn Francis. *Judging Jehovah's Witnesses: Religious Persecution and the Dawn of the Rights Revolution*. Lawrence: University Press of Kansas, 2000.

Pietila, Antero. *Not in My Neighborhood: How Bigotry Shaped a Great American City*. Lanham, MD: Ivan R. Dee, 2010.

Trepagnier, Barbara. *Silent Racism: How Well-Meaning White People Perpetuate the Racial Divide*. 2nd ed. Boulder, CO: Paradigm Publishers, 2010.

Magazine Articles

Anonymous. "Yellow Peril." *Newsweek*, February 20, 2012, 5.

Bartz, Andrea. "Accidental Bigotry: Racist Behavior Emerges in the Absence of Actual Racism." *Psychology Today*, November–December 2011, 10.

Bentley, Rabbi Philip J. "Bigotry Is Treif! [not Kosher]." *Moment*, May–June 2012, 11.

Bosman, Julie. "The Case of Loving v. Bigotry." *New York Times Magazine*, January 1, 2012, 39.

Fallows, James. "Just for the Record: Anti-Mormonism Is Bigotry Too." *Atlantic*, October 9, 2011. www.theatlantic.com/politics/archive/2011/10/just-for-the-record-anti-mormonism-is-bigotry-too/241444/ (accessed June 21, 2012).

Koenig, Darlene. "Give Bigotry No Sanction." *Teaching Tolerance*, Spring 2012. www.tolerance.org/magazine/number-41-spring-2012/give-bigotry-no-sanction (accessed June 21, 2012).

Saletan, William. "Be Nice to Bigots." *Slate*, February 14, 2011. www.slate.com/articles/news_and_politics/frame_game/2011/02/be_nice_to_bigots.html (accessed June 21, 2012).

Sullum, Jacob. "Hate-Free Hate Crime: Dharun Ravi Trial." *Reason*, July 2012, 13.

Teitel, Emma. "Uniting under the Bigotry Umbrella." *Maclean's*, January 30, 2012, 11.

Organizations Counteracting Bigotry, Intolerance, and Hate

Numerous organizations work to eliminate bigotry and hate. Only a dozen are listed below with brief descriptions taken from their websites, as well as their addresses and phone numbers:

American-Arab Anti-Discrimination Committee "is a civil rights organization committed to defending the rights of people of Arab descent and promoting their rich cultural heritage," according to its website.
1990 M Street, NW, Suite 610
Washington, DC, 20036
202-244-2990
www.adc.org

American Civil Liberties Union says it "is our nation's guardian of liberty, working daily in courts, legislatures and communities to defend and preserve the individual rights and liberties that the Constitution and laws of the United States guarantee everyone in this country."
125 Broad Street, 18th Floor
New York, NY 10004
212-549-2500
www.aclu.org

Anti-Defamation League "fights anti-Semitism and all forms of bigotry in the United States and abroad through information, education, legislation, and advocacy."
605 Third Ave.
New York, NY 10158
212-885-7970
www.adl.org

Asian American Legal Defense and Education Fund "is a national organization that protects and promotes the civil rights of Asian Americans."
99 Hudson St., 12th Floor
New York, NY 10013
212-966-5932
aaldef.org

Gay, Lesbian & Straight Education Network "is the leading national education organization focused on ensuring safe schools for all students."
90 Broad Street, 2nd Floor
New York, NY 10004
212-727-0135
www.glsen.org

Leadership Conference on Civil and Human Rights "is a coalition charged by its diverse membership of more than 200 national organizations to promote and protect the civil and human rights of all persons in the United States."
1629 K Street, NW
10th Floor
Washington, DC 20006
202-466-3311
www.civilrights.org

National Conference for Community and Justice "is a human relations organization dedicated to fighting bias, bigotry and racism in America."
1095 Day Hill Road, Suite 100
Windsor, CT 06095
860-683-1039
www.nccj.org

Parents, Families and Friends of Lesbians and Gays "promotes the health and well-being of lesbian, gay, bisexual and transgender persons, their families and friends through: support, to cope with an adverse society; education, to enlighten an ill-informed public; and advocacy, to end discrimination and to secure equal civil rights."
1828 L Street, NW, Suite 660
Washington, DC 20036
202-467-8180
community.pflag.org

Sikh Coalition "is a community-based organization that works towards the realization of civil and human rights for all people. In particular . . . towards a world where Sikhs may freely practice and enjoy their faith while fostering strong relations with their local community wherever they may be."
40 Exchange Place, Suite 728
New York, NY 10005
212-655-3095
www.sikhcoalition.org

Southern Poverty Law Center "is a nonprofit civil rights organization dedicated to fighting hate and bigotry, and to seeking justice for the most vulnerable members of society." The organization publishes *Teaching Tolerance* magazine, which provides help for educators who work to help students appreciate diversity.
400 Washington Ave.
Montgomery, AL 36104
334-956-8200

Stomp Out Bullying "focuses on reducing and preventing bullying, cyberbullying, sexting and other digital abuse, educating against homophobia, racism and hatred, decreasing school absenteeism, and deterring violence in schools, online and in communities across the country."
220 East 57th Street
9th Floor, Suite G
New York, NY 10022–2820
877-602-8559
www.stompoutbullying.org

VOX Teen Communications "is a non-profit youth-development organization located in downtown Atlanta. . . . VOX has enabled thousands of metro Atlanta teens to express themselves freely through *VOX Teen Newspaper*."
229 Peachtree St., NE
Suite 725
Atlanta, GA 30303
404–614–0040
www.voxteencommunications.org

Index

About the Author

Kathlyn Gay is the author of more than 120 books that focus on social and environmental issues, culture, history, communication, and sports for a variety of audiences. A full-time freelance author, Kathlyn has also published hundreds of magazine features, stories, and plays, and she has written and contributed to encyclopedias, teachers' manuals, and textbooks. She is the author of a number of titles in the It Happened to Me series: *Epilepsy* (2002, with Sean McGarrahan), *Cultural Diversity* (2003), *Volunteering* (2004), *Religion and Spirituality in America* (2006), *The Military and Teens* (2008), *Body Image and Appearance* (2009), and *Living Green* (2012).